RESCUE TO RECOVERY

A VETERAN'S STORY OF HIDDEN SCARS AND PERSONAL DISCOVERY

TRACEY BROWN

First Printing, 2020

Book Cover Design by Sofia Booth
Illustrations by Ashlyn Smith
Interior Book Design by VMC Art & Design, LLC

ISBN 978-1-7349604-0-2
Library of Congress Control Number 2020907444

Printed in China

TABLE OF CONTENTS

ACKNOWLEDGMENTS

This book has been a long time coming. There is a very long list of those who have been a part of the journey—I thank you all, as it really does take a village. There are a few people I would be greatly remiss if I did not thank by name. First and foremost, my mom, Judy Brown Schaefer. You have ALWAYS been my rock, my encourager, my biggest cheerleader, my sage and yes, comic relief. Thank you for always accepting me and loving me for who I am, no matter where I am on this journey. To my sister, Kelly Brown Smith, you are my hero, my first and forever friend. Words will never be able to convey my gratitude for your constant love and encouragement. To my niece, Ashlyn, you have no idea how you have affected my need to "figure shit out." You are so talented and kind, a true empath. There is an amazing connection we have, and I am extremely grateful for you. I thank God every day for you three. I thank God for my other family: Ron, Michele, Dominique, and Sofia. I am forever grateful for you and how much you have been a part of saving my life. You gave me purpose when I didn't think

I had any. Thank you to my high school friends for reconnecting and helping me to remember so many lost memories. To my friends who are family, my "tribe," thank you for just loving me no matter what and providing endless laughter. It is so necessary. Thank you Jo and "Doc" for getting me connected with Veterans Affairs.

To my sailing tribe, unbeknownst to you, every time we got on the water you were and continue to be a part of my healing. Thank you.

Thank you to Tam Luc for teaching me how to put this whole journey into words and to the amazing counselors at Veterans Affairs in Long Beach, CA.

The journey continues...

INTRODUCTION

R escue to recovery is a window into a United States Coast Guard swimmer's life in the early 1980s. It is a journey that many veterans and first responders find themselves on after serving. Trauma comes in many forms, and it is not reserved for the first responders. For those who *do* choose to step into harm's way or to help in crisis or devastation, it is even more common. Although trauma and its effects have been, in years past, somewhat of an enigma, there has been more and more understanding of how it affects the human psyche.

This book is not a clinical look at trauma. It is not diagnosing anyone or claiming any particular ways to heal trauma. It is a picture of decades of a life suppressing pains, and the personal discoveries that led to more freedom from those pains.

After serving in the Coast Guard and after many difficult years, I studied to be a director of rehabilitation. I began working with my chiropractor and helped to build his physical rehabilitation facility. He took me under his wing and, in essence, continued my education in the healing arts. With this education and years of specializing in scar tissue, many light bulbs went off regarding the scar tissue on my soul.

This book is my journey of understanding the confusing and frustrating characteristics of trauma and the challenges of overcoming stigmas and my own judgments. Working as a physiotherapist I realized the similarities between physical and emotional trauma, and thus began a journey to reconnect my life.

I have many hopes for this book. I recently connected with my close high school friends, and Leslie, one of my best friends from those years, said that at our ten-year reunion people came up to her and asked "Where's Tracey?" or "What happened to Tracey?" Well, of course she didn't know. In reality, "Tracey" didn't know either. One big hope is that this book will help explain to my friends and family where I have been for the last thirty-plus years. Why my interactions at times could be abrupt or strained. Hopefully it will help others to understand and will further the conversations of personal trauma. Perhaps it will shed some light for others who have been "different" after devastating loss or repetitive trauma.

My hope is that these stories and some of the lessons learned might help lower the defenses for those who feel the need to "stay strong" in the midst of their own pain. I hope this book will help those who have been the helpers, heroes, and warriors to understand that some of the strengths and gifts that make them so good at what they do can also hinder their healing from pains they have endured.

My hope is that this book will help people to connect some dots in their own lives that they may have difficulty connecting right now.

My ultimate hope is to give hope. Hope to those who feel as though they have been so lost that no one will ever find them. I was there and felt that same lostness. There is hope and there is help.

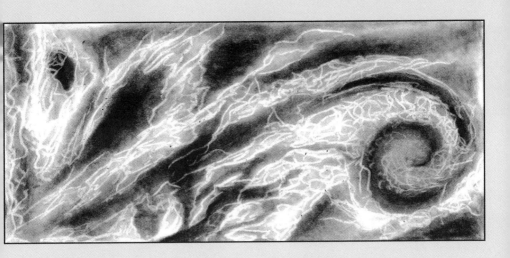

CHAPTER 1

You Don't Know What You Don't Know

hange—how many stories and emotions can be created and attached to this one word? There are times in our lives when we know we need to make changes. Sometimes we need to change jobs, sometimes it's a need to move to a different location or change relationships. Sometimes, such as where I found myself, it seems like *everything* needs to change. I was at a place in my life where, if I were to compare it to an injury, my injuries were critical, the life-support kind of critical, and I needed to make a change. Even more importantly, I was *ready* to make a change.

It took a very long time to realize that my inner world was on life support. I had become quite adept at compartmentalizing my life, to the extent that some areas didn't even seem real anymore and some, so long ago, seemed as if they had never happened at all. Even though I had a wonderful family and great friends, all of them kind, fun, caring, and encouraging, I had this constant agitation and an underlying belief that I was this terrible person. I felt as though I had done something wrong and was continuously filled with an overwhelming feeling of shame. As I checked in with myself during this time, I realized that I was having a very hard time remembering events in my life. I was unable to concentrate or see things through to completion. The smallest things would irritate me more and more. I was depressed, I was exhausted, and yet, I couldn't sleep without aids.

These feelings were always just below the surface, easily aroused, although most of the time I was able to bury them by sheer volume of activity. By staying busy, I kept the noise of the world louder than the noise in my head. I played the "I'm doing great" card very well, so well that I almost believed it myself—almost. From the outside I really looked like I had it all together. I was physically fit, I was working hard on my new business, I smiled and seemed genuinely engaged. Most of the people at this point in my life didn't know I was ever in the United States Coast Guard or even what that meant. It's not that I wasn't proud of my military service, I just didn't think it mattered. It seemed so long ago that I didn't think anyone would actually care, and I certainly didn't have any context by which to insert that bit of information. I also didn't have a lot of patience in those days, so I didn't have the energy I imagined it would take to get someone up to speed on what I considered an old storyline anyway. If ever I did, I would quickly tell a funny story or make a difficult story funny. Humor has been a great defense mechanism for me. I would never tell the sad stories or the gruesome stories, the things that no one needs to have in their mind. Things I wish I didn't have in mine.

So, I would go to the parties, go to the family gatherings, do "things"—anything. I would work out, "do" life, but inside I felt like I was dying. I felt as though any bit of my former happy, joyful personality had all but disappeared. It was getting harder and harder to find the energy to be with others or, for that matter, even get out of bed. Every endeavor I would begin, time and time again I would lose momentum, lose energy, be completely overwhelmed, and I would stop it before it had a chance to really take off. I felt so very emotionally distant from everyone, family and close friends, to the point that I was utterly numb. In situations I would take a supporting role in someone else's endeavors. I would be the support crew, the background singer, the person behind the scenes.

The years in the Coast Guard had brought about some profound changes. Yes, those were some natural years of growth. I was almost twenty-two when I went into the Coast Guard and about twenty-six when I got out. Four years in a life, a long time ago, but twenty-five-plus years later, the effects still haunted my soul. One day, the light bulb lit up and I needed to make a change.

The "light bulb" was a social media post by a friend of mine almost a decade ago. She had posted sixteen characteristics of post-traumatic stress disorder. I'm kind of an information hound so I was very interested. Not that I thought it had anything to do with *me*, I just thought it was interesting information. It was an "aha" moment, or more like an "oh shit" moment. I was living with fourteen of those sixteen posted characteristics and so many more, as I would come to learn. This information hit my brain and I literally sat staring at that information somewhere between disbelief, relief, panic, and wondering where the reset button was for my mind. If I wasn't totally numb before, I certainly was now, now that I had this information. So, I did what I thought any normal person would do. I filed that information somewhere else in my brain and went on with my day. Funny thing about truth, though—once you hear it, you can't unhear it. This information was now in my head and it was wreaking total havoc with my emotions. Looking back, it was a seed. It was the beginning of the end of the "long winter of my soul."

Change is a funny thing. When I decided to go into the Coast Guard I made a very conscious decision to shift my life 180 degrees. Little did I know *how* that would shift my life so many years after that decision. But we'll get into that later. Here's the thing: When you truly decide to make life changes, expect *a lot* of things to change.

Not so much the little things. I realized that little shifts here and there actually tended to make little changes, which in hindsight was good for someone who did not do change easily. I was about to change my life drastically and at the tender age of twenty-two I had no idea what I was in for, which was, again, probably a good thing. I didn't know what I didn't know. It's one of those sayings that makes perfect sense after the lesson has been learned. I knew I was going to change locations, I knew I was going to learn things, but in my very early twenties, I had no idea how these short four years would impact and change literally everything about my life from then on.

When you're looking to make big changes in your life and character, expect not just *you* to change. Everything changes. Sometimes people and their attitudes change, sometimes locations are permanently changed, the people with whom you spend the majority of your time can change. There's a great saying by the late Jim Rohn: "Things don't change, we change. Things don't get better, we get better." Thank you, Jim Rohn. So when we decide to make changes, please *expect* things to change because, in reality, we will change. We will learn, grow, get hurt, and certainly be changed as we move through this life.

Change can be really scary for some people. If I were to look at my life even fifteen years ago, I really wanted things to be different, but I was not ready or equipped to make changes. Looking back, I don't think I even knew that I had actually changed all that much. Once I realized I needed to really look at myself, it became clear to me that if I didn't shift my life choices I would not get better and, therefore, nothing else in my life would get better either. I had to take the initiative and make a choice to either stay in the pains of the past, or take steps towards a better future. We always have a choice even when we don't think we do. Five years after getting these hints of needed change, I saw the post from my friend. It took a few more years to actually *be* ready for change.

When I left Los Angeles for boot camp it was January in the early 1980s, eighty-five degrees out, and a beautiful sunny California day. When I landed in Cape May, New Jersey, it was very late, dark, and twenty-five below zero. That should've been my very first indication that things were never going to be the same again. All I could hear in my humor-twisted mind was the phrase from *The Wizard of Oz*, "We're not in Kansas anymore."

I have learned since those days that change is one of those things that is a constant. We are always in flux, we're always adapting, if we choose, and hopefully we are ever evolving. Many times we are not that conscious of changes. Our character changes sometimes drastically and quickly and sometimes subtly and slowly. Sometimes we initiate change through education or other means. Sometimes outside forces or insults to our psyche put us on high alert and that, over time, will change our character. I use the word insult because when there is a trauma, blunt force or otherwise, in the world of medicine and healing, insult is used to cover a wide range of incidents and accidents. There are many ways our hearts and emotions are molded. Some for better, some not so much. The good news is, for those wounds that no one sees, there are tools and resources available to begin the healing for all who want them.

Acknowledgment was for a very long time foreign to me. It wasn't a comfortable concept. Another one of those "I didn't know what I didn't know" kind of things. Who knew the healing capacity the simple act of acknowledgment possessed. To be sure, I did not. I never understood how important acknowledgment was until I started examining my life as a veteran. Just using the word veteran alongside my name is foreign to me even though it's been over thirty years.

When I first separated from the Coast Guard, I called Veterans Affairs seeking guidance for a home loan and my medical benefits. When I called I was told that I didn't have any benefits, they couldn't "find me" in the system. I thought this odd because I *did* serve my country and when I enlisted I was told that I would have benefits upon separation. But the people I spoke to on the phone—and there were several—told me repeatedly that I did not have benefits, I was not in their system. Little did I know that this would be yet another brick in the wall and would affect my life profoundly.

This hiccup, as it were, was all due to another "you don't know what you don't know" moment. I had come to believe that those at Veterans Affairs were the end-all authority and that they knew what they were talking about. To be fair, from the standpoint of those I spoke with, they were correct—I was not in their system. Let's pause here for a moment.

Had I known and had I been less fragile in my emotional state to ask a few questions, perhaps this episode of my life would have set a different course for the next thirty years. Note: Questions are good. The military teaches us not to ask questions, we are taught to follow orders. They teach the questioning out of us, that is, enough to create a cohesive unit without descent. I have learned that most of the time when communicating with others, no one has the whole picture. We are all blind to what we don't know. And in this case, I didn't know what I didn't know. I didn't know I had to go through a process to transfer from the active duty military system to the non-military system of Veterans Affairs. The person on the other end of the phone didn't know that I didn't know that. One could argue that they should have, but apparently there were a lot of missteps at the VA in those years. This all being said, because of this one seemingly small detail, I began questioning the years that I served. In fact, as things began to spiral in my mind, I questioned a lot of things. I questioned my reasoning powers, I questioned my life memories, I questioned my worth, and due to many emotional insults, I questioned the meaning of my existence at all.

Once, in a seminar, I heard a profound statement. "What I say to you is something, what you say to yourself is everything." When there is a lack of acknowledgment from other people, our inner dialogue can get skewed. We have great power by simply acknowledging others. Think of the homeless. They are just as human as you and I, yet how many times do we walk by without even the slightest hello or eye contact acknowledging their presence?

What we say to ourselves—our inner dialogue—is extremely

important, and much of that is built by the acknowledgment and encouragement of others. For the longest time I truly felt like an island. No one knew my pains, and no one knew the things I had seen and done. For years I didn't even acknowledge to myself, let alone others, my pain and shame because I had come to believe that I didn't matter.

The truth is, the only way to see or be seen is to at the very least acknowledge our self, our pains, fears, and experiences, as well as acknowledging others around us. Brené Brown has said that the "only way back to each other is by seeing and being seen." Many times in my life this "being seen" would only happen, and rarely, by a kind friend pushing and probing, not by something within because there was no way I was about to expose what was going on in my head and heart. That stuff was dangerous to me, I couldn't imagine what it would do to a friend, friendship, or family. I literally would rather jump out of a perfectly good helicopter before telling someone about my fears, short-comings, uncertainties, depression, or my inabilities to cope.

For many years I avoided allowing others to get close enough to look at me. I avoided allowing myself to be seen. As rescuers or warriors, being vulnerable creates a weakness in our armor. While doing search and rescue, my mindset was that of invincibility. Out in the water, me against the elements, my mindset was, "I've got this." Seriously, I'd better have this or it will have me. But invincibility does not translate to matters of emotional insults. I can honestly say the mask of invincibility is a self-imposed prison sentence. It is a sentence of isolation and completely unsustainable. We are social beings, we are beings created to be in relationships, and those relationships either fortify us or break us down. When invincible and unwilling to be seen, relationships don't go deep nor do they last. I had put a limit on what I would allow people to see and over time my world got smaller and smaller.

People can build us up or tear us down and, yes, what we think is very important and what we say is even more important. If we do not have or allow others to acknowledge us, encourage us, see us, I guarantee that the discouragement of even silence will kill the greatest of spirits sooner or later. The older I get the more I realize how much I really don't know. When I was seventeen I "knew" everything, no one could tell me how to guide my life. By the time I was thirty it was getting clearer how little I knew. And by the time of this writing I'm in a place in my life where "you don't know what you don't know" is more of a mantra. A motto, to stay open. Open to input, open to see and to be seen, and open to new adventures of my mind and emotions.

CHAPTER 2

Obstacles

O bstacles, challenges—we all have them. Some seemingly more difficult than others. When rescuing victims, most of the challenges I faced were ones I could see. I could see what the weather was, I could see how big the swells were, I could deduce the probable physical condition of the victim by what the weather and water conditions were, as well as how long they had been in those conditions. Many obstacles were available for some kind of assessment. There were, however, factors that my colleagues and I could not see. One major obstacle we could not see immediately was the reactions the victims would display when we approached or began the process of either getting them off of their vessel or out of the water. The obstacle of the victim's state of mind. We were taught how to ease panic to some extent or confusion in the victim on the occasions they were disoriented. We were given some psychological tools to assuage the natural reaction of a victim to seemingly insurmountable obstacles.

I can remember one rescue of an older man. Mind you, older is relative. I was in my early twenties at the time, so older to me at that point could have been forty-five years old. We did not know how long he had been in the water, but it was long enough for us to work in the belief that he would either be hypothermic or possibly even unconscious. The water in the San Francisco Bay is always cold. Obviously colder in winter. I remember that day thinking I'd probably be warmer in the water. There was about a three to four-degree difference in temperature between the air and water, the water being warmer.

Obstacles—that cold water was definitely an obstacle, not just for our victim, but for me as well. I knew I only had so much time before I would be greatly restricted in my abilities to help this man, before hypothermia started to take hold of my mental and physical faculties. Although I had a survival suit (more on that later), I still didn't have a lot of time. We were able to get pretty close to him so I didn't have to spend too much time in the water while getting to his location. The first thing we were taught to do upon approach to a victim was to state our name and tell the victim we are with the United States Coast Guard and that we are there to help. We say this in hopes of helping the victim calm down. I mean, after all, if you are in a very dangerous and scary situation it might be reassuring that an expert in these types of situations is there with you. This man taught me a great lesson that day—even though I told him I was there to help him, he was not at all happy to see me.

First, let me say, he was scared. He was a big guy. He was moderately hypothermic, which means shivering had stopped and he was a bit confused. We had big swells as per usual at that time of the year in the Bay, and the conditions were not getting any better as time passed. I asked him a few questions like what kind of boat he owned, if he was married, just some questions to get his mind off of the dire situation.

I will never forget his reaction to me. He didn't seem to be relieved that the Coast Guard was there to help him. In fact, he actually got angry with me. I understood from trainings that uncontrollable panic can be a reaction when someone is really scared. As a swimmer, we were taught to keep some distance from the victim as we would approach them in the water, because they can actually drown you by jumping on you or crawling on you while you are trying to rescue them. But he wasn't doing that. He was just mad and it was specifically due to me being there. Now, I was young, but in my mind I was thinking, *I AM THE UNITED STATES COAST GUARD. Come on, dude, I'm here to get us both outta here before it gets really nasty, and you're givin' me attitude?*

I came to a great realization years later that in this extremely dangerous and scary place (life-threatening, to be sure), this big guy, who by this time was completely helpless, became angry because I wasn't the package he expected. I believe that when he saw this little girl (I'm five foot two on a good day) swimming up to him saying, "Hey, I'm here to help…" he must have thought, *Great, now I'm really screwed.* The lesson I learned years later is that in the midst of great obstacles or challenges, sometimes our way through does not come in the packages we might expect or desire. It can be humbling. I'm sure he would have liked to have seen some young, strong, stud of a guy out there to get him to safety. It would have been much easier for a forty-some-odd-year-old man to handle in the early eighties. But no, he gets this feisty little girl. It had to be a hard pill to swallow. The good news is, after much ado, I was finally able to get him in a basket and out of the water to warmth and safety.

I reflect on that rescue often when facing obstacles or great challenges. More often than not, the answers or the help we need will come from very unexpected places or people. I had fears when I realized I needed to change things in my life. I think that perhaps they were some of the same things that man feared during and after his rescue. Things like embarrassment and shame for being in that predicament, how people would look at him or judge him after he was rescued, and then there's that whole being rescued by a girl thing. Not the package that he expected or desired.

The stories we make up in our heads can be crippling. My belief for years was that my biggest obstacle for moving forward in my life was my inability to communicate the confusion going on in my mind, but in reality the true obstacle was fear. I had so many fears swirling around in my head. Yes, I did fear that I would be unable to untangle the webs of uncertainty that were created over such a long time. I was afraid to trust anyone with my emotions. I was afraid that if I were to let someone in I would either scare them away or no longer have the strength of will to accomplish anything in life. And yet, I was ashamed of where I actually was in my life, that I couldn't fix my life, and admitting that was even worse. I was in a prison of my own judgment because of the stigmas I had associated with seeking help. Perhaps some of those storylines went through that man's mind, that he couldn't get out of that predicament on his own and now some little girl says she's there to help. Maybe that's why he was mad at me for being the one to rescue him. Sometimes injuries, accidents, and misfortune can trigger feelings of shame or self-judgment.

Many of the obstacles in my life were so powerful that some dreams remained dreams and were never realized. Obstacles that kept me playing small. For me, this rescue helped me to understand that one of the first great obstacles I needed to overcome was my belief that I had to figure out how to rescue myself. Like where that man was, alone, cold, confused and in a very angry ocean with no resources. After years of floating around in my lonely ocean of emotions I came to the realization that I truly was unable to rescue myself, and the shame that came with that was enormous. It created an anger in me, anger born out of frustration. I can relate to the frustration that man had, the inability to "fix" his situation.

The more I delve into the "whys" of the trajectory of my life (i.e., joining the Coast Guard), the more I am fascinated at the subconscious and creative ways I have learned to relieve my pains. When I was a teenager, if someone were to describe me they would have said things like outgoing, daredevil, or risk taker. In those days, adrenaline junkie was not common vernacular, but that was what I was. The faster I went or the higher a cliff to jump from into water, the better. I was an absolute thrill seeker. There are reasons why people do the things they do. I realized later in my life that I had some things spoken over me, things spoken to me early in life that set my mind as a child into a belief that gave me the impetus to do crazy things.

A very early trauma in my life presented a lot of challenges and obstacles. I realized later in life through some great teachers that for most of my life, I had formed a belief that I didn't matter. Like I didn't belong here, not just in situations or places but that I wasn't supposed to be here on earth at all. It wasn't a passing thing. It was so deep and so real that it invaded every aspect of my life.

When I was eight years old I was burned very badly. I was hospitalized for months and doctors were not sure if I was going to make it. In an early memory while still in the hospital, I was just out of a coma and a few of the statements I heard my doctors and nurses constantly say were, "It's a miracle that you are here," or, "This is amazing, you shouldn't be here," or, "I can't believe you're here." These statements spoken to me, meant to be an encouragement, in my little eight-year-old mind turned into a very literal statement that I shouldn't be here. Somehow in my young mind the seed of not belonging started to take hold, and even though I had some divine encounters and a loving and kind family, these seeds began to grow. I mean, back then what the doctors and nurses said was gospel, right?

By the time I was a teenager, that tiny seed of "I shouldn't be here" had grown into a big obstacle of "I don't matter" and, therefore, the conclusion was it really doesn't matter what crazy things I do because what's the worst that can happen? I could die, but that really didn't matter because I shouldn't be here anyway, I should have died when I was eight. (Teen logic is not logical.)

One of my favorite sayings these days is "Don't should on yourself." I should do this or I should do that. We get enough of that from others. I wonder how many people—especially these days in the world of keeping up with everyone, social media, and TV—feel the weight of just not belonging. There seems to be such great disconnect these days and the feeling of not belonging. The mere disconnect because of social media is enough to push some to the outer edges. It is a heavy burden not to belong.

I have recently learned that traumas can build upon each other. So the time I spent in the hospital at the age of eight set a stage for that "small" incident with Veterans Affairs when they could not find me in their system. The confusion in my mind about not being found in their system, and the inability to communicate that I really did belong in the system, was a continuation of the seed that was planted long ago. It wasn't anyone's fault. I mean, lying in that hospital bed so many years ago and with the limited understanding they had of burn victims, it really was a miracle. They were as surprised as anyone that I really did make it, and today I can accept that and hear it for what it is—a great blessing. Yes, I did have some counselors when I was burned and they helped with the outward scars to the extent that my young mind could grasp, but the internal ones were just beginning to grow.

The human psyche is intricate and fascinating, kudos to all who work with it as a profession. Some people process trauma and stress very quickly and it passes through them and out of them. Some are very courageous and look at it head on immediately and they recovery beautifully. Thankfully post-traumatic stress is recognized more these days than back then. When I separated from the Coast Guard they did not do a psychological evaluation. They do that now. We are in some very informed times and there is much help available. But the saying that "you can lead a horse to water, but you can't make it drink" still rings true. The word "help" still has a stigma to many. It did for me and I can only imagine how many others, especially those who are used to being the rescuers, warriors, and helpers.

It is fascinating to me that we will go to a doctor or hospital in a minute when we break a bone or something really doesn't feel right in our body. So what is it that stops us from seeking help when something doesn't feel good in our heart or mind? Shame and fear, whether acknowledged or not, kept me from so very many things. It kept me from reaching out when something was "off" in my mind and heart. Shame, as I said before, was a great obstacle for me. I would say to myself so many times "I should be over this by now" or "I'm fine" and I would bury whatever I was feeling. Everyone takes on trauma and stress differently. I think I chose to go into the field of physiotherapy because I really like helping people feel better (partly because it helped me for years to ease my own pain) and because anatomy makes a lot of sense to me, it has a logic to it. Those in psycho-therapy have my greatest respect.

Speaking of logic, for an emotionally healthy adult the conclusions I reached as a young person were not all that logical. In the very young, not-quite-developed mind of a traumatized child, adrenaline-filled activities were a great release, not a good idea, but somehow helped me to feel alive and temporarily relieve some of the emotional/mental pains. It gave me something to focus on rather than the noise in my head. Doing extreme things demands focus, and it created relief—if for only a short while.

If I could talk to that little girl today I would do my best to help her understand that there is no judgment when it comes to fear or pain. There is, however, great relief by allowing others in and talking about those fears and pains. Adventuring out to the boundaries that hold us back from achieving dreams can be scary, great adventures usually are. But freedom from the pain and heartache is on the other side of that adventure, an adventure you will not go on alone. Right now you don't understand but when you are ready, little one, it's an adventure that is there for you to take.

CHAPTER 3

How We Function

mentioned briefly that I am a physiotherapist. I specialize in scar tissue. Scar tissue is a big deal. According to research, every wound (e.g., after an accident, disease, or surgery) results in some degree of scarring. Scar tissue is confused tissue that replaces normal tissue after injury or insult. Scar tissue lacks elasticity and blocks regeneration of healthy tissue. Some believe that ninety percent of pain and lack of mobility in the body is due to scar tissue. That is a big number.

Scar tissue has other interesting characteristics. It has a numbing effect and, untreated, it may not stop growing until it completely immobilizes the injured area which in turn will affect areas around the injury. Scar tissue is not as sensitive to touch as healthy tissue, that is, from the viewpoint of the person with a scar. Scars on the outer surface of the skin get less information from the nerves, and so, when someone touches it, it feels numb, dead, or some say it just feels "weird."

I have often heard from clients who had very old injuries that the pain went away from the initial injury a long time ago, so they thought it "healed" itself, only to realize years later that their body simply figured out how to function around the injury. The end result with untreated injuries is sooner or later the affected area will slowly stop functioning properly. It will lose its full range of motion and it will lose strength. Sooner or later that area will shut down, completely ineffective, and not just that area, but any area that is a support will be affected. Every muscle group around an injury is affected by the injury. The body is not isolated in its components. Every part of the body is connected someway and somehow. So no injury is an isolated event. When I am with a client, I have to take every muscle or joint, every ligament or tendon in the muscle group into consideration as to how they were affected by this insult.

That said, the human body loves to heal itself. What I mean by that is when you give it the right stuff, the right nutrients, water, sleep, exercise, therapy after injury and proper structural position, the body is incredibly engineered to heal itself, but it needs all the right components. Scar tissue is a natural response to an injury. It's the body's way of isolating and immobilizing the area in order to heal it. I have had many injuries while doing search and rescue and as an athlete. I did what many of my clients have done after an injury—I ignored the pain. Not because it didn't hurt, or because it wasn't significant enough to keep me from doing my job, my fear was that I would be marginalized or "benched" and not allowed to continue my service. I was also very young and "invincible" and certainly not as wise as my now older version of me. I wish I had known then that the sooner I addressed and treated those injuries the better off I would be years later. I am fascinated at how fear has been a constant roadblock for me, and yet I was not willing, able, or perhaps aware enough to admit it. I absolutely believed that I had no fear. Nothing was too outrageous or scary because I wasn't afraid—that is, in the physical realm.

Part of the reason to treat injuries as fast as possible is to minimize the discomfort and pain, but the long-term reason is to keep the body from doing what it does naturally—that is, create scar tissue. The body would happily immobilize or shut down the area and forget about it. Emergency averted and it can get back to doing what the body does. Without intervention or treatment, the body will do what it can to protect itself from further insult. The most important of all things to the body and mind is protection. Survival at all costs. Losing function of a limb is a small price to pay for the whole body to survive. However, the body does have warning systems. Pain is a warning system, an indicator that something is wrong. When it comes to pain, a signal from the injured site is sent to the brain via the nervous system, screaming SOMETHING IS WRONG. Our initial reaction to pain is to not move that particular area and hopefully seek treatment. Sometimes that pain can be so impressive that we may not engage in activities that could replicate the same circumstances from which that injury occurred. This is a very natural emotional reaction to physical injury or insult. So warning systems are very good to have, they are there to keep us from danger.

This warning system of pain is not reserved for blunt force trauma alone. This same system is in place when it comes to an overuse injury. Overuse injuries or overuse syndrome will create the same effects as blunt force injuries except that these injuries occur due to repetitive motions or insults. I have heard statements from clients more times than I can count that sound like, "I just woke up and I couldn't lift my arm," or, "I just bent down to pick something up and my back locked up for no reason." When it comes to pain or an inability of a particular part of the body to function, there is always a reason. This is when, as a therapist, I would have to get forensic. I would have to ask a lot of questions regarding what my client does for work, are they an athlete, do they recall any accidents or injuries? Most people think it has to be about something that happened recently. I would ask them to think about old injuries and most of the time their reaction would be surprise because there is "no way" something from twenty or thirty years ago was affecting them today. If there were no injuries (very rare) then I would inquire about things they would do repeatedly. In many instances, the combination of an old injury and repetitive motions around an old injury could create the problem for which they were now seeing me.

For example, I have worked with a lot of athletes, and they can have a host of issues from the repetitive movements needed to hone their skills. These issues range from tendonitis to a loss of strength or the complete loss of range of motion in a joint or limb, and sometimes they would simply have chronic pains. A very common issue with students and office workers is chronic neck pain due to constantly working on a computer or improper ergonomics while sitting at a desk. Looking at what a person has done or does on a constant basis helps me to understand and determine where the injury could have originated.

Once I am able to understand the motion, the repetitive movement, or the history of that person's injuries, it's fairly simple to put a treatment plan together for recovery. Many times, I must add, if there is no repetitive cause, getting to the source of the pain is more difficult because the client doesn't remember the injury. This can be due to many factors, how long ago it occurred or them thinking it was no big deal and left it to "heal itself." Note: Injuries do not "heal themselves," we learn to work around the injury. Our bodies figure out how to compensate for the injured area. Muscle groups in proximity to the injury are recruited to take up the slack and, at some point, they too begin to break down or shut down.

Our emotions have a protection mechanism as well. Something traumatic can block out our memory of the trauma, and it can also block out other memories. As if the brain shuts down at that very moment, it's like a reboot of a computer but only some of the information that was on that computer was erased. It's frustrating because there is no rhyme or reason to what information is lost. I know all too well as I have very few memories of my childhood before I was burned.

When it comes to repetitive emotional trauma the effect is the same as that of a singular devastating incident. Repetitive emotional trauma can induce a loss of emotional range of motion, or it can induce overreactions to emotional triggers. But because there was no one incident to point to, it's hard to trace the origin. It was absolutely frustrating, confusing, and depressing for me to not know why I reacted the way I did or, just as frustrating, to not be able to react "appropriately" in different situations.

"Fight, flight, freeze" is another one of our warning systems that we will go into more detail on later, but the toll on the psyche from repetitive insults can be crushing. I believe most first responders and those who are repeatedly in harm's way are in a constant state of controlled fight, flight, or freeze. This warning system is extremely important to keep us alert when in danger. Once the danger has passed it is meant to shut off. One way to help fight, flight, freeze to shut off is to talk about the traumatic experience. We know this now. However, back in the early eighties, this was not standard practice. We would debrief on cases regarding what went well and what didn't and how to improve. We would write reports, but discuss feelings? Not a chance. One thing that has been so fascinating to me as I learn more and more about trauma is that at the time, I don't think any of us thought that the many particularly difficult and heart-wrenching missions were even affecting us. We were just doing our job.

Experts have learned from veterans and first responders that repeated traumas build upon each other. Without discussions or a way to process what was seen, heard, and felt (or, at the very least, acknowledgment of the insult) we are left with a large void in our psyche that we can't really describe.

For me, I didn't have the understanding, the tools, or a system to process the things I saw. As I stated earlier, I didn't even know that I was being affected by what I was trained to do. When I got out of the service I just felt numb, bored (for lack of adrenaline), confused, ashamed, and actually embarrassed that I didn't know why I was feeling what I was feeling, nor did I have the coping skills I thought I "should" have to cope with those feelings.

Overuse syndrome in the physical world and repetitive trauma in the emotional world take the same toll. They create scar tissue that restricts our range of physical motion and "e"motion. It creates pain and ultimately, without treatment, will shut that traumatized area down. In the case of emotional trauma, that shutdown can look like numbness, confusion, anger, irritation, sleep disorders, poor concentration, isolation, panic attacks, shame, guilt, fear, and a host of other things I never thought were related.

When I joined the Coast Guard my number one reason for joining was to help people. I was eager to serve and go somewhere to be a part of a great team and tradition in service, to be a part of something bigger than myself. I truly felt that I had signed up for saving lives and making a difference for those in need, and yes, we did save some lives, but in reality, on small boats, we did many more recoveries of bodies than rescues of victims. The repetitive insults of rescues turning into recoveries created a lot of emotional scar tissue that went unaddressed.

For a very long time in the field of physio and physical therapy, if someone had a very old injury or had extensive scar tissue the chances of them getting big gains in recovery were slim. The technology we had was old and it was a very slow road to healing. The advent of lasers became very promising but was extremely expensive. I was fortunate in a twisted way to have been injured while sailing. I severely tore my rotator cuff and was pretty sure I would need surgery. But I chose to do as much work as I could with what I knew to avoid surgery, as I was very aware that even surgery had its drawbacks. After nine months of traditional therapy, I was about seventy-five percent better. Range of motion was OK, there was still pain but it was manageable. I said to the doctor I was working with that there had to be a better way. "Certainly with all the technologies in the world we should have more options than the barbaric practices of breaking up scar tissue and ultrasound." With some time and effort researching we did find a great tool that, as strange as it sounds, uses high frequency vibration to reorganize scar tissue. This was fascinating to me. It "reorganized" scar tissue after insult or injury. That took some time to sink in.

This concept of reorganizing scar tissue was a complete break-through for me as it not only helped the healing of my shoulder but was instrumental in making the connection in my emotional healing as well. The concept of scar tissue being *confused* tissue made perfect sense to me and helped to answer some of my deeper questions as to why my emotional range of motion was restricted and why my heart was shutting down. It helped explain why I was numb to events and interests. I realized that these injuries, these insults, put my psyche in a confused state and simply needed to be reorganized. Not that this is a clinical explanation of post-traumatic stress or that it is "simple", but it did speak a language I understood. It helped me look at my own confusion and emotional state in a different way.

Now, this may seem very simple or elementary to some, but to me, it was revolutionary in that as I mulled this concept over in my mind each day working with my clients, the stigma that I had about emotional therapy began to fade. I'm not going to say I was excited to do therapy, and at that time in my life I had no clue as to where to begin that process. But one of the great obstacles I'd had—the stigma, my attitude about asking for help—had been adjusted, and that was a great step in the right direction.

I have been in what some would consider very dangerous situa-tions, I have been through perils, physical pain, and downright crazy circumstances. Oddly, these perilous times were almost comfortable to me because, after all, back then I didn't think I mattered. But the choice to do this emotional work in the scary place called my mind was more frightening than anything I had ever done in my physical life thus far. My mind and emotions were the great unknown. Most of my life I felt as though if I were to go "exploring" as to why I was the way I was, I may never come back. Fear, that great obstacle, the creator of "what if?" How many times did that question keep me from opening up to someone?

Once I was able to make the connection between physical scar tis-sue and emotional scar tissue and how very similar they are, I became hyperaware that I had a choice to make. It is the same choice every athlete or warrior has after physical injury. The choice to do the work, to work through the pain, through the frustration and inconvenience, to do whatever it takes to get back to a healthy place from which to live and function at my greatest capacity. It is a choice to look at what my reactions are and why I have those reactions or lack of reactions and the choice to address them. It is a choice to allow myself to be exposed for the sake of my greater self. It is a choice to step into a very unfamiliar and uncomfortable place. And looking back, it was a very good choice.

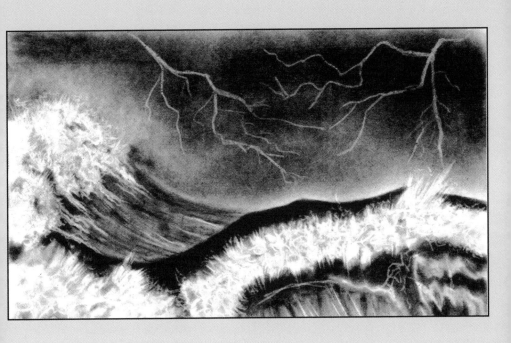

CHAPTER 4

Being Brave

I magine you've been getting beat up by an extremely agitated ocean for hours while on your forty-one-foot rescue boat. It's pitch black outside, the seas are getting rougher and seemingly blacker as time passes (if that were even possible). The air temperature with the windchill is insanely cold, and the water…well, the water is actually just a bit warmer than the air. You're standing on the edge of the boat, you're in your survival suit that is two sizes too big, time seems to be going in slow motion, and your skipper (coxswain) is not so patiently waiting for you to jump into the abyss.

Did I say it's pitch black out and the water is black? Yeah, the only light I could see was from the spotlight held by my engineer. A very high-powered spotlight that created a shimmer on the water in hopes of keeping the person we were there to rescue in sight. My survival suit… OK, we'll call it that. It was the early 1980s and at this point in history, women were not exactly welcomed by the old "salts." Many times I would overhear these guys saying things like, "Women are bad luck on boats," (what century were they in?) and, "Women can't do what men do." Yet, here I am, the only woman on the crew and one of the very few women Coast Guard swimmers and I'm about to jump into these cold waters in a men's medium wet/dry suit. The point of a wet/dry suit was to let the first round of cold water into the suit. Once the water was in the suit it was to stay in there and my body heat would warm it up. Great in theory. However, with the suit too big, I had constant cold water coming into my suit and nothing warmed up. Very motivating, though, to get in and out of the water as quickly as possible.

We did all of our preparation work for how we were going to orchestrate this rescue, from assessing the victim to how to get him on board depending upon his abilities. All medical kits were at the ready, we'd gone over the contingency plans seemingly a thousand times. In this instance, everything is going through my twenty-three-year-old brain like lightning. This was my first time as the sole rescue swimmer on board a forty-one-foot utility search and rescue boat.

I'm in the San Francisco Bay, just inside the Golden Gate Bridge. Outside of the bridge and a bit to the north are the Farallon Islands where there is a very large contingency of great white sharks. And now, just before I jump into the water, all I can hear in my young impressionable brain is the oh-so-familiar sound of the nearing shark in the movie *Jaws*. Dun dun…dun dun dun dun… Yeah, you can hear it too. If sharks happen to show up, my coxswain is at the ready with an M16 semi-automatic rifle to shoot it before it gets to either me or our victim (yeah, there's that, sharks and M16s). Not comforting. And still, I have to jump into the blackness.

I found myself in a mental game of listening to my coxswain saying something about when am I going to be jumping into the water, trying to turn down the *Jaws* theme which is actually getting louder in my head, and all the while trying to convince myself that this *is* my job *and* what I signed up for, so I need to find whatever I need to find inside of myself to just jump into the dang ocean.

That moment of finding whatever I needed was a moment of truth, also known to some as a "come to Jesus" moment. I was a newbie on this crew. I was also the first woman these guys had ever had as a rescue swimmer and this first jump was the platform from which I would find out if I had what it took to do this job. It was the moment my crew would find out if they could trust me when it was all on the line. In a matter of a minute or two, I had to check in with myself and truly check in with my faith. It was me alone and no one else jumping into that water that night. I had to trust my preparation, my training, my physical ability, and mental fortitude. I had to fight my natural instinct to move away from this crazy moment, and I had to trust my crew to keep an eye on me. Oh yeah, and hope the coxswain had good aim. Ready, set, jump!

That moment was surreal on so many levels. On one hand it felt like everything was in slow motion, and on the other hand it felt like everything was going at the speed of light. Being on the water at night is very different than during the day. Things look different, it feels different, and there is another level of trepidation simply because depth perception is skewed and your bearings are just a bit off. Some might call what we were doing brave, some *have* called it crazy, and those of us who did it daily called it duty. It's what most of us signed up for, what we trained for, and just what we did. We went out to those in need or in peril and almost always in the most undesirable conditions.

I believe there are a couple of different kinds of brave. Being brave in the moment is one thing. Sometimes we have no choice but to be brave. Due to circumstances, we step up to be in the space to save someone, physically or emotionally. Sometimes the moment is so instantaneous that being brave simply happens as a reaction. How many heroes have been born out of this instantaneous bravery, and thankfully so. What I've learned, not to diminish the heroism, is that instantaneous bravery can sometimes be simpler than what I call intentional bravery. I understand that instantaneous heroes feel the pains of the incident just as much as anyone. What I'm saying here is it is not natural to choose to step into something knowing full well that there will certainly be pain and danger and possible injury or even death.

The natural order, the instinct of most animals, humans included, is to stay as far away from pain or danger as possible. And it's not necessarily the physical pain of something that hinders us in the long run. As a Rescue Swimmer, when I intentionally jumped out of a helicopter or out of a boat, I knew it was going to hurt physically. There have been times just before hitting the water that I knew, *This one is really gonna hurt.* The physical pains might be minor, bruises were common, some injuries were a bit more severe, but the physical pain is pretty temporary even if you sprain something or break a bone. Physical injuries are part of the deal. The lasting injuries, those that lasted beyond the years of search and rescue, the invisible injuries and scars that no one could see that came along with each of those "rescues", the constant assault on my soul, these ultimately haunted me for decades.

Helpers, heroes, and warriors are really good at stepping in to rescue others who are in danger or distress. It's what we are trained for and, for whatever reasons, at that moment in time we have the mental fortitude to do it. I believe one of the reasons is the ability to compartmentalize, the ability to set our safety aside for however long its necessary in order to focus on the task at hand, the safety of another. We are able to disconnect our emotions from the situation. I call it the superpower of the first responder. To me, it is this superpower that gives rise to the ability to function at a very high level during a crisis so as to get ourselves and others out of harm's way.

I believe that everyone has a superpower of some kind, but this ability to disconnect is a factor that sets first responders and warriors apart from other people. I am not comfortable with the word bravery when it comes to what I did back then because, at the time, it really was my job.

Over time, I found that this ability to disconnect was not just a big factor in being able to do my job well, but it became a very big factor in the delay in recognizing the symptoms and characteristics I had developed. I had become very good at disconnecting my emotions from most everything due to the repeated traumas of rescues that turned into recoveries, of being just a minute or two too late and someone dying moments before we arrived, the countless recoveries of bodies that were released from the deep.

The symptoms of post-traumatic stress were subtle. It's not like one day I woke up and said, "Hey, something's wrong." It was more like days of lightness and joy became fewer and farther between. My attitude and demeanor especially after a particularly painful case would get very dark. My humor, which for years was a shield, got extremely dark. I truly lived "work hard, play harder" to the fullest, and play hard usually included a lot of alcohol. A coping mechanism to try and forget what I went through while on duty because just disconnecting after a while wasn't keeping this stuff out of my head. These insults were intruding on my daily conscious and interrupting my sleep. Nightmares became the norm, so alcohol and sarcasm became good friends of mine.

After a while I started to believe that I was just not a very nice person. The subtlety of these characteristics are such that I really didn't know what was happening to me. Yes, I was young, in extreme situations, and everyone was dealing with these insults however they could. The only way we would communicate about any of this stuff was with humor, trying to make light of the horrible things we had to see and deal with. A couple of the guys had to do rehab for alcohol, and one of the guys was on medication that was supposed to make him sick, violently sick, if he were to drink even a beer while on the meds. Not this guy, he could drink anyone under the table all the while taking his meds. Looking back, we really had no clue as to the damage that was being done to our psyches. It truly was a very different time, all of us just trying to cope however we possibly could.

It's been decades since that first night. Decades since those days of trials and testing to see if I could cut it. It was a big deal to be accepted as one of the boys. It was a very big deal on future missions for the other crew members to actually want to be on another mission with me and to trust me. It was a big deal then and it is still a battle for women to be seen as equal. To be sure, we are innately equal to men.

There are situations where some women are not as strong as men and I have been in situations where men are not as strong as women. But if we are prepared physically and have the proper training mentally and intellectually, then there is no reason to keep a woman from putting her "name in the hat" for any task for which a man is otherwise allowed to apply. I have always said that if I or any woman got the opportunity and our name got drawn to do something not traditionally done by a woman, we'd better be completely prepared, mentally *and* physically.

There was something else I learned. Those men on my crew were just as scared as I was that first night. Not just because it was an insane night to be on the water, not just because the waves in the Bay were big and it was cold, but they had a rookie, a female rookie, whom they had to trust. This was a long way from their comfort zone, and it's not like they asked for the girl to be on the crew. I was assigned to that boat and they were very brave to comply with those orders. Again, this was a very different time in history, we all had a lot of skin in the game and we were all standing in our own type of bravery.

Bravery comes in many forms and it's not reserved for the rescuers and warriors. Bravery is the single mom or dad getting it handled any way they can. Bravery is the first day at a new job or learning a new skill, it is the mom and dad who deal ever day with their child who has a life-threatening disease. Bravery is taking another shot after failing again and again, or reconciling with a friend, family member, or loved one after a miscommunication or after feeling betrayed. Bravery is all around us. For some it takes a tremendous amount of bravery to just get up out of bed every morning, or to go to sleep at night. For me, I can honestly say that one of the bravest things I ever did when I realized I was ready was take a deep breath and ask for help.

CHAPTER 5

Stories We Tell Ourselves

When it comes to search and rescue as well as being an athlete, repetition is a great trainer. It is a part of any great training plan. While being a part of a search and rescue team, we had drills that we would do daily in order to stay sharp. Drills such as a mock victim in the water where the "victim" was part of our team and their goal was to do something that was out of the ordinary so we would have to use our training, use our ability to change our plan of action, and strategize when something did not go according to plan. Note: Rarely in search and rescue does anything totally go "according to plan."

We did weapons training constantly so that when a time came to use our weapons it was committed to muscle memory. Training prepares the mind and muscles to be ready so we did not have to *think* about drawing our weapon. We would simply react due to constant repetition of training our muscles simultaneously with our minds. Learning any new skill, even one as simple as riding a bicycle, is repetition. Yes, it is simple now, and we can do it without a thought, but that is all due to repetitive training so we don't have to think about doing the task. We start with training wheels at first, then in doing the movements over and over we master them, and then eventually we are riding on two wheels like a pro.

When we do something physically over and over again, we are not only training our body but, as mentioned, we are simultaneously training our mind and emotions. The power of repetition cannot be overstated. This concept of neuronal pathways in the brain, once only theory, is now being documented. Doctors and researchers are able to show how "habits" are created via repetition. Habits like riding a bicycle. The brain creates these pathways that are so strong that we can do them without thinking. Repetitive trauma works in the same way.

There is a lesser used word when it comes to training our bodies. One that tends to have a negative emotional attachment. In times past, when I would hear the word failure or even think about the word failure, it would trigger so many emotions and reactions or it would cause me to react and retreat inward and not want to interact with others. But failure is actually good when it is allowed to be part of a healthy process. When I am working with a client on physical training or rehabilitation, after making sure they are structurally sound, our goal is to gain strength, so we work a muscle to failure repeatedly. Taking a muscle to failure tends to garnish the greatest results. It is very important that the structure is sound before we begin the process of rebuilding the muscles' strength. Working muscles to the point of total exhaustion, using every ounce of energy stored in that muscle, creates great gains.

Repetition in and of itself *is* a great teacher when it comes to building muscle *and* our subconscious. Doing something or having something happen to us over and over creates pathways in the brain just like any other repetitive action, which creates habits and, might I add, reactions. Good and bad habits are most often learned through repetition, and when we add negativity or a negative experience or emotion to it like pain or anguish, we can create some detrimental storylines in our minds. What I have come to believe is that these new negative pathways can break down an otherwise sound emotional structure. When it comes to negative outcomes due to a negative subconscious thought process from these new pathways, it becomes easier to see how we can spiral negative thoughts through our mind to create an isolated life.

In boot camp, the goal of the company commander is to build a cohesive unit. The very first impression after the flight from Los Angeles to New Jersey was getting herded onto a bus bound for Cape May. There were eighty people or so from all walks of life on that bus that cold late January night in Cape May. There were kids from Boston to California, New York to Florida, all of us were between the ages of eighteen to early twenties. We had vast differences in upbringing, values, experiences, emotional structure, and intelligence. I would say that night we had one thing in common. The minute that company commander came onto the bus and started barking out orders, every one of us was scared and confused and literally went into fight, flight, or freeze so our brains basically shut off. Some of these "kids" never got out of fight, flight, or freeze the entire eight weeks of boot camp—some of those kids who were on that bus that night did not graduate with the rest of us.

I think about those kids and what it was in their upbringing or in their subconscious storyline that was different from those of us who had finished. What stories went through their minds while some crazy guy with a huge voice went up and down the aisle of that bus yelling instructions? What was it in their emotional structure that initiated the enlistment but when BIG stress, disorientation, and extreme physical and emotional demand entered the picture they couldn't complete the course?

I know, for me, I was fortunate. My mom was my greatest cheerleader and encourager. Whenever I had a challenge or something was hard for me growing up, she was always there to remind me that I can do anything I put my mind to, and I truly believed her. She set me up with a very sound belief system and emotional structure. I could hear my mom's voice in my head so many times while at Cape May. "You can do anything." This was repeated so many times in my life by my mom that it was deep in my subconscious so that it didn't matter what the company commanders and powers that be threw at me. I believed with everything in me that "I can do this!" Nothing these people do or say can break my spirit, my will, or determination.

It reminds me of that saying: "What I say to you means something, what you say to you means everything." My mom started this dialogue before I was in the hospital as a little girl—what she said to me became the words I would say to myself. She planted the seeds of ability and optimism, and she watered those seeds continually as did others as I grew and became an accomplished athlete. By the time I was in boot camp I believed I *could* do anything, certainly anything the guys could do. I believed I could conquer any obstacle course, any swimming drill, and any mental challenges. I could complete any kind of endurance testing simply because I believed that I could.

On the opposite end of the spectrum I have found that when I have been inundated with negative input, losses, or failures and constantly barraged with physical insults or emotional insults, my mind is not as strong or confident. The years of search and rescue, with intended rescues that turned into recoveries of bodies, time and time again, this repetition of failures or perceived failures had a profound effect on the script that my mom had so diligently created in my subconscious. My feelings of ability and accomplishment diminished greatly. Subsequently, so did my confidence and outgoing spirit.

Our brains are wired to find patterns and create stories. Our brains are always, whether we are aware of it or not, constantly looking for these patterns and stories. Patterns that help to calm and stories that fit our inner dialog. This is where repetition of the negative kind can really get a hold of our emotions. Even someone with a strong inner dialog can, with enough negative input (both physical and emotional), be susceptible to the pains of trauma. Our brains are so wired for stories that if there is not a complete story, we will make one up. Have you ever sent a text to someone and you see the response bubbles...waiting... waiting...and if your wait is long enough you start making up stories about what they are thinking? I know I have.

There were times when the storylines going through my head were totally negative, about my worth, my abilities, my losses, etc. In those days, if during a conversation with someone they would say something with a negative tone or they would have a reaction to something in a way that triggered my inner negative storyline, my reaction was almost always defensive or even explosive. My reactions of course depended upon how severe the trigger was. I lived a totally reactionary life. My subconscious storyline had been changed so severely that if I thought someone was being the slightest bit off in a conversation, I could make up a story in my mind that fit my subconscious state and my reaction would be completely out of proportion.

This explosive behavior was happening to me more and more. I had so many negative stories going on in my mind. Stories about how I had failed to get to a victim on time, how I failed to save a life, failed to get to the scene on time, how it seemed that most every case we went on somehow failed, this constant negative input. These repetitive traumas overshadowed the truths that were my bedrock and the truths that we did save some people and that some of the cases we went on did have positive outcomes. It's amazing to me how powerful constant negative input is. These insults, these traumas that were compounding, had completely rewired my brain to believe that I was worthless, that I wasn't capable, or that I was a huge failure. They had changed the once sound structure of my emotions to the point where I had no confidence or self-esteem. One of the hardest things was that I really didn't believe in myself anymore. It was as if the traumas I had endured had replaced any trace of the things that my mom, friends, family, and actual accomplishments had taught me.

Boot camp is a petri dish for the militaries to find out who can withstand immense stresses, both physical and mental. To find out how each individual will function at those very high levels of stress, with an added bonus of limited sleep and uncomfortable living conditions. The thing about boot camp, though, is it has a limited timeframe. We had a saying at Cape May: "I can do anything for five minutes," or however long a drill might last. "I can do anything for an hour or two or three." When there is a time limit, most anyone can somehow stay the course and endure. The Coast Guard back then was very proud to have a sixty-five percent fail rate. Meaning sixty-five percent of every class that came into Cape May did not complete the course and were sent home.

Boot camp is one thing, a short time of controlled risk and ever-increasing stress testing. But in the real world of search and rescue, the constant barrage of painful, dangerous, soul-wrenching scenarios with no end in sight is another. I do believe that *not* talking about these incidents or dismissing them, compounded with the numbing agent of alcohol, helped to keep those traumas inside of me. Buried, but ever present whenever they were unknowingly stirred up. I trained myself to cope with the memories by not talking about them, pushing them way down inside, avoiding anything that would remind me of that time. I stayed away from a place I loved—the ocean—for more than twenty-five years because instead of it bringing me joy, it only brought me pain. This once happy place would too often bring up memories that would induce depression or nightmares. So I just stopped going.

Definitions are very important to me. Unfortunately, when it comes to life and death situations, failing to succeed in a mission can be devastating. Failure can truly mean the end of someone's life. The loved ones and those who were assigned to keep that from happening bear the extreme pain, guilt, and loss due to that "failure." When this happens over and over, the weight of that pain and guilt over time becomes unbearable.

There are some positive notes here. One of the exceptional qualities of failure is that it does create opportunity for feedback. I lived for years, as I would imagine many have and still do, believing that we are only as good as our last performance. Back then it was my last rescue, which was few and far between recoveries. Some people truly live and die by the fact that they either win or lose, succeed or fail, with failure being the great inferred disgrace.

I have, as of late, come to embrace the notion that failure can be a positive thing. It can help us to grow and become better. We seldom get as much feedback from winning or succeeding as we do from losing or not succeeding. And so I have come to understand that I can choose to write a different story about failure. I can choose to put "failure" into the category of "tools." Just like any other tool, it is there to help accomplish something that without it would be very difficult if not impossible to do. Emotionally, the more tools I have, the faster I learn, grow, and become a better human being overall. I have come to realize that it's not a matter of losing or winning, but truly all experiences are tools to help us learn and grow.

For so many of my early years, the saying "you can do anything you set your mind to" was my battle cry for everything I did. Every physical activity I was able to accomplish was due to setting my mind to do it. This was a great story in my mind and heart and was key to all my achievements. Doing things like jumping out of a boat at twenty-five knots or out of a helicopter, or life things like learning a new language or taking on a new job, were all a question of putting my mind to it.

For years I thought I could use this same approach in the context of healing my emotions. There was one particular problem with that though—I didn't have the tools within myself to create the changes I so desperately needed. I didn't have the same kind of mental fortitude I once had. The foundation or structure of my youth, that "fearlessness" I once had, was shaken so profoundly and in a way that was completely foreign to me and beyond my ability. For so many years I kept telling myself, *I can get through this by myself, I can figure this out, I just need to set my mind and do it, I can do anything, why can't I do this?* But I wasn't able to "get over it" no matter how I tried by myself. I didn't have the understanding or the tools I needed for this job. I would get so frustrated with my inability, which would once again feed the negative story of incompetence or that I was worthless so I would go back to what *was* working and avoid anything that would bring these feelings up. I would just shove these feelings down a little further every time and try to "muscle them away." And then, as years went on, my world got smaller and smaller, meaning things I once enjoyed lost their appeal and I would stay home more, shutting people out more and more. I started "shoulding" on myself more. "I should be over this by now." "I shouldn't react to these little things." "This shouldn't be such a big deal." "I should go out more." I should, I should, I should.

I have found that, yes, mindset is extremely important. But just as it is with the physical body, if I am to try to build strength after an injury, I need to make sure the structure is sound before strengthening it. If it is not structurally sound then I'm only going to be training in an improper position and set myself up for another injury. It is the same for the inner being, the emotional world. When it came to my mind, my emotions, I needed someone or more than one to help me get my emotional structure sound again. I didn't have the tools needed to create that structural restoration. I didn't understand how trauma works on the psyche and how traumas build on each other. Once I realized that this was what I needed, it made the decision to ask for help that much more manageable. Realizing that retraining my brain was the same as retraining my body after an injury made this so much more tolerable for me, and the stigmas of asking for help slowly fell away. Again, I'm not saying it's easy, I am saying it is a simpler process than I had created it to be. The hard part was getting all the made-up stories about "help" out of my way so I could actually ask for help.

The stories I had created around the word failure and the stories I told myself about my worth and abilities, the stories about asking for help for my mind and heart, were all just made up. I told myself all kinds of stories that simply were not true. Big stories and not so big, from "I'm not good enough to be loved" to "I don't need anyone to help me I can do this myself." Not true for me or for anyone. We are not created to walk through this world alone, and certainly not through retraining our emotional state.

I had to, as they say, come to the end of my rope and actually admit something before I could rewrite the stories I had repeatedly told myself. I had to once and for all admit that—surprise, surprise—I could not do this on my own. My emotional structure had been compromised. And so, just as I had done so many times before with physical injuries and physical structural damage, I decided to "do the work." I decided that I would seek out help for my emotional injuries and insults. I also decided that I would not quit. This is an ongoing process. Not that I am so broken I'll never be fixed, but more to the point, I want to continue to grow as a person and be a better person today than I was yesterday, every day. And this takes a commitment to do the work, daily. So in choosing to do this work, I found that I was able to start telling myself some new stories. Stories I could start telling myself because of the compassionate people who chose to help those who ask. Those who are trained to go into that *scary and dangerous* world of the mind and emotions. Like I said before, this was scarier than jumping into pitch-black water in the dead of night where sharks roamed free. This work was and is the only thing that stood between the pain-filled, small, stunted life I was living and the wide-open world of limitless possibilities I once believed in.

Once I decided to reach out and trust someone who knew their way around trauma, to my surprise, things began to change. It took a long time to change my story around the word failure and to give it another meaning. It took a long time to realize I was not alone, that I was not crazy and that I didn't have to, nor could I, do this alone. It took a long time to be worn down by my own inner thoughts and to become completely numb. Another surprise, it didn't take much time to begin to feel relief from the pain, relief from the guilt and shame, and to begin to see for the first time in a long time that there is more than this one-dimensional world of darkness and confusion. I began to learn that there are others who have the same thoughts and feelings from similar experiences. There is hope, and not only hope but there is actually fulfillment and joy that had been lost to me for so many years. Time to do the work and not stop until….

CHAPTER 6

Fight, Flight, Freeze

Operational training. First responders do a lot of training, as you can imagine. It is the most important part of "the work," to train your mind and body to be able to respond quickly and consciously in emergencies. The work is preparation, physical training, learning new and better ways of doing things. The work is also gathering tools, physical and mental tools, to make our job easier and more effective.

Athletes do physical training to enhance their sports performance for speed and endurance. "Mathletes" train their brains for faster and faster mental performance. First responders train to enhance our physical response and reflex times as well. Muscle memory is a lifesaver for first responders. The difference between someone who consistently trains their mind and muscles to do a task and the person who doesn't can be the difference between surviving or not. We train not only to increase speed and mental capacity but, perhaps even more importantly, to ensure our ability to perform under pressure and stress. There is this condition that we have touched upon called "fight, flight, freeze." It is a natural response to imminent threats. It is the body's automatic, built-in system designed to protect us from threat or danger. It is critical to our survival. The problem with fight, flight, freeze with first responders is the catastrophic effect it can have if it engages during a mission. So, we train.

We train our mind and muscles so they will respond without thought, hopefully overriding the fight, flight, freeze responses. This training buys us precious seconds of decision making and trained reactions which could help save the lives of victims as well as ourselves.

One such training session has stayed with me vividly since the day we did the exercise. It was a typically cold, early spring San Francisco day. The wind was less than usual so we had the opportunity to do some training with small boats and a helicopter. We were using the three-meter zodiac surf rescue boat along with one of the helicopters from Air Station San Francisco. The drill we were engaged in was a "simple" victim in the water in need of a basket hoist to the helicopter. In order to do this, one would pretend to be a victim, the other would be the rescuer, and then the helicopter crew would lower the basket on a cable. The zodiac was there for safety and to practice picking a victim up without the basket. The way it was *supposed* to work was the rescuer would go through all protocols just as if it were real. "My name is Joe Swimmer, I'm with the United States Coast Guard, and I am here to help you." Ask questions. "Are you hurt?" Ask the victim's name and help get the victim oriented if they are not. Again, the training is the same every time, repetition, to make sure we are always training the mind and muscle on the same exact things to minimize the effects of fight, flight, freeze. Remember, *we* are in the water as well and it is a dangerous situation. We as responders have to fight the fight, flight, freeze response just as everyone else. Repetitive drills, putting memory in the muscles, and becoming adept in stressful environments give us a bit of an edge on the grips of fight, flight, freeze. That is, if all goes to plan.

It's my turn to be the "victim." I'm in the water and the zodiac is close as usual. There is a rookie in the helicopter on the hoist cable, it was his first time hoisting—what could possibly go wrong? The rescuer gets to me and goes through his protocol, he gets me into the basket and makes sure the basket closes properly. When the cable is taught, it pulls the top of the basket closed which helps to keep the victim from falling out of the basket while being hoisted. It's not an easy feat to get a victim into the basket, let alone a fake victim like me in full survival gear. It's also not easy with a real victim as they may or may not be coherent and they are sometimes combative. So I'm now in the basket, the rescuer signals the rookie in the helicopter to begin to raise me up and…pause here for a moment.

This guy is a rookie we are training so all of us can become better at our job. My partner and I, the ones in the water, we've done this several times before. This kid in the helicopter is doing his very first live training. He's nervous as one can imagine *and* he literally has our lives in his hands. Training for rescues can be just as dangerous as real-life rescue situations. In the rookie's nervousness he forgot to change the orientation of the levers in the helicopter from lower basket to *lift* basket, so instead of lifting me up towards the helicopter, he drops the basket with me in it, deeper into the water. A simple mistake, his brain wasn't thinking clearly. However, this simple mistake sets off a chain of events that could have been disastrous.

I was fortunate to have some seasoned Coasties all around me. The guys in the zodiac immediately see what's going on, as does my partner who is close to me in the water. They all quickly jump into real-life rescue mode as if it were second nature (training). They move towards me in the basket. Now, the basket is going under water. However, it has buoyancy so it doesn't go all the way under but goes under just enough so I can't put my head high enough to breathe. The kid in the helicopter is now in a bit of a panic (he does have supervision up there, thankfully). The helicopter crew figured out what he'd done but then, all of a sudden, the cable from the helicopter to the basket gets caught up in the propeller of the zodiac's outboard motor. The crew in the zodiac are ON IT, and what seems like five minutes is most probably all of thirty to forty seconds, all the while I'm holding my breath (literally). The guys in the zodiac along with my partner make quick time of getting the cable free from the propeller just in time for the rookie to start hoisting me up to the safety of the helicopter.

This fight, flight, freeze reaction, again, is a very normal reaction to stressful situations. Our training and all training for high-risk work is imperative to hopefully bypass the fight, flight, freeze response, if only temporarily. It is some of the most important work we do. Preparing for any and all situations. That rookie got a good taste of what can happen when the thinking part of his brain shuts down even for a second.

We observe fight, flight, freeze when watching a scary movie. As the audience, we are saying, "Run!" and the person in the movie is just standing there. That's the "freeze." Or, just the opposite, when someone is hiding in a movie and they just bolt and start running, "flight." We, in the movie theater, see the situation in its entirety and are not stunned by fight, flight, freeze, so our brains can reason. However, when in a panic, the rational part of the brain shuts off. One person might run, one might freeze, and many times as a rescuer we see a lot of the fight part. When we approach a victim they tend to get combative in the water because they can't run or freeze/hide. People can get disorientated as well, our mind is not functioning at its full capacity when in the midst of a fight, flight, freeze response.

Fight, flight, freeze is essential for survival. All animals are wired to experience this response, it is unconscious and automatic, it is NOT a choice, and each person's body has their unique way of responding. Fight, flight, freeze on a biological level is fascinating as well. Blood starts pumping to big muscle groups (your heart starts pounding) and blood pressure increases. Hands get cold and clammy. Breathing becomes fast and shallow, or one can hyperventilate to increase oxygen to the muscles so they can keep moving. Muscles get tense, ready to spring into action. Pupils dilate to take in more information, to see better. Fear and anxiety increase, one is "on edge" or high alert, ready to move if need be. The thinking part of the brain shuts off and it becomes hard to think clearly. We don't need to be reasoning or planning, we just need to survive, get out, run, fight. Tunnel vision is another characteristic of fight, flight, freeze—all we are looking for is a way out. One reaction I thought was very interesting is that our digestive system shuts down. No blood going to the stomach as it is needed elsewhere. (Many who suffer from post-traumatic stress tend to have digestive issues.)

Everyone experiences fight, flight, freeze, whether for a few days or weeks after a threat or trauma; however, the response is meant to turn off once the threat has passed. Post-traumatic stress can rear its head in several situations: exposure to life-threatening situations, repeated traumas, prior traumas that were not addressed and then built upon with the next trauma. When someone has been isolating or avoiding anything that reminds them of those traumas, that is when we see long-term issues. I have mentioned some of the things that post-traumatic stress can do to a person. The lack of sleep and the avoidance of anything that is a reminder of that trauma are the number one and two factors that keep post-traumatic stress going long term. If we don't express the pain or anxiety, it will stay in us and can create great dis-ease within.

There are two primary changes that happen in the brain involved in post-traumatic stress. The first is that the fight, flight, freeze response stays on; it doesn't turn off after the trauma as it should. The brain continues scanning for a threat and the person suffering may not even be aware of what is happening on a subconscious level. For some, a trauma—or repeated traumas—sends the part of their brain that turns on fight, flight, freeze response into overdrive.

In other words, the brain can no longer tell the difference between actual danger and reminders of danger, it all registers as DANGER. As was taught in a class at Veterans Affairs, think of a smoke detector that is sounding that screaming alarm all the time. It has lost the ability to detect when there is actual danger, it can't tell the difference between steam and fire, so it is on all the time. Consider how exhausting it would be if the smoke detector in your house was on all the time.

Would you be able to focus? Would you feel irritable? Would it be hard to sleep? The switch never turns off for those of us who are experiencing post-traumatic stress and, therefore, we are in a constant state of high alert and most are in some state of sleep deprivation.

The second change in the brain is "thinking" turns off. The part of the brain that controls thinking, planning, and decision making turns off. Reasoning and higher thinking are muted. Of course, when there is real imminent danger, we don't need to think and sit around planning, we need to react, we need impulse, and we will be willing to take more risks to survive. We don't "think it through," we just react.

These two changes were happening in my brain. I began realizing that I was not reacting to small irritants the way friends and family reacted. When fight, flight, freeze is turned on all the time, it is not only difficult to think clearly or concentrate, it also means that I couldn't think through the best way to respond to a situation. Instead, I would just react based on the fear, anxiety, or anger I was feeling in the moment. There was a knee-jerk reaction to most any irritant. This was compounded by the lack of sleep, as it is with most people who suffer from post-traumatic stress.

I'm sure everyone at some time or another has been sleep deprived. Moms and dads with a newborn, *that'll keep you up.* Working the graveyard shift or swing shift and finding it difficult to sleep during the day or during off hours. Stressing over finances, health, or relationships. Lack of sleep is such a huge factor when it comes to irritability. This is unfortunately very common for many people, as well as for those dealing with post-traumatic stress.

Do you ever awaken from a very deep sleep and for a time you are so disorientated that you may not even recognize your own bedroom? It's like you know you're awake but your brain is not quite functioning and you almost feel like you are in a dream? Or you might be awakened during an emergency and you can hear someone's instructions and move about and follow those instructions because there is nothing physically wrong with you, but as far as making critical decisions, you are almost paralyzed. This was my world as I became conscious of the way I reacted to exterior stimuli or my inability to tolerate mild emotional irritants. Semi-functional in every aspect of my life. Able to listen and understand information, but really struggling with critical thinking around certain emotional situations; it was debilitating. I have described the feeling as when my computer has that little wheel on the screen while it's "thinking" constantly spinning but the screen is stuck—blank. My screen (brain) was stuck, spinning and trying to find the information within to have an appropriate reaction to that which was happening around me.

In this semi-functional state of being, this awakening period, I tried to build a business on my own while trying to be in a relationship, and on top of that, trying to be present and of service to family and friends. I say "try" as I was "there" physically in those settings (not always, sometimes I really just couldn't muster the energy) and doing everything possible to be present and effective. The underlying problem was that I didn't have near enough energy to be and do all those things simply because the "alarm" was on full blast.

While building my business I would attend seminars, and at one of those seminars I remember a speaker who told a story that went something like this:

Imagine every day you wake up and you are handed ten balloons. Each balloon holds one tenth of the energy you have for the day. That is all the energy you "get," ten balloons. Now let's say you didn't get a good night's sleep, pop one balloon right off the bat. Then, let's say you have a disagreement with your significant other, pop another balloon. How about your rent is due and there is not enough money to cover it, pop another balloon. Let's say upon getting to work your boss gives you a real hard time about something that wasn't even your fault and won't let it go, pop another balloon. Work is piling up on your desk and all you can think about is a sick family member, pop another balloon. You essentially used half of your energy and it's not even lunch time. You have five balloons left to get you through the rest of your workday and to get you through your evening at home with your loved ones. If you have kids, a loved one who might be sick or other people who count on you, these are all stressors that take energy to address—balloon poppers. By the end of each day you may be tired, but a good night's sleep and you are good to go for the next round of balloons.

For many of us who experience the pains of post-traumatic stress, a good night of sleep is a dream. I know that was true for me. Sleep for many, many years was not something I looked forward to. In fact, I would stay up till the wee hours of the morning because I was terrified to go to sleep. I had such nightmares when I would fall asleep that I would wake up with night terrors, sweating and in a panic, or in some cases I would wake up crying, reliving the lost lives on my watch. I was beyond exhausted, I felt like there were just not enough balloons to even begin each day.

I'm sure I'm dating myself, but do you remember the television show called Hogan's Heroes? If you don't know the show, it was a comedy about World War II prisoners at a certain German prison for allied forces (sounds strange, but true). The prisoners were actually feeding information to the allies as they would gather it from the German guards and higher ups. The prisoners had an escape tunnel. That's how they were able to get the information to the front lines. This tunnel was small and confined, little room for a couple of people at a time. It went underground from the prison, under the fences, and opened up in a forest outside the prison, essentially freedom.

For a very long time after my years of service, I felt as though I were stuck in the middle of that tunnel. I remember describing this tunnel to a friend at one point, literally saying that I was so deep in this tunnel from trying to push traumas out of my mind or trying to avoid reminders of them that I didn't know if I was walking back towards the prison or towards freedom. When in actuality I was pushing myself deeper and deeper into my own prison, that of isolation. My world felt like that tunnel, small and confined.

I have learned that the prison is real, and I have learned there is a tunnel that leads to freedom from that prison. And the biggest lesson I have learned was that I had to make a decision to ask for help because this kind of healing necessitates someone outside of the self. One of the many reasons—and it's a big reason—is because with post-traumatic stress the brain is still in fight, flight, freeze and the thinking part of the brain is turned off. Part of this healing is to stop hiding or avoiding, stop pushing the pain away. I wanted to stop denying myself of speaking my truth or experiences and start expressing—physically, emotionally, and intellectually. It was, as with the beginning of any great adventure, that a decision must be made and action must be taken. I used to tell a joke about changing a light bulb: How many people does it take to change a light bulb? Just one, but the light bulb has to want to change.

CHAPTER 7

A Different Kind of Brave

've said this before, change and I did not get along at all. Although in reality life is a series of ever-moving parts, the discomforting thought of change in my inner world paralyzed the fluidity of my outer world. I became very good at scheduling my life. It gave me a feeling of order. Having a job, the schedule of when to get up, go to work, take lunch, and go home is a structure and is comforting. I think part of the reason much of the repetitive traumas didn't begin to surface earlier for me was due to so much structure while I was in the military. There was little civilian stimulus and that translated to everything being "normal." The schedule of duty kept me in this comfort zone, and most of the people I associated with were military people. We all had a commonality of military life.

I recall, within the first year of separation from the Coast Guard, two initially very strong feelings that I vacillated between were that of being lost and that of being bored. When I was discharged I had some "vacation" time. In truth, I didn't have a job. Looking back, there was so much unscheduled time, so much time inside my head reliving so many scenarios and no tools to process those scenarios. I could understand the aspect of being lost. Just as much as life changed 180 degrees when I entered the Coast Guard, there was another big shift when I left. When it came to being bored, it makes sense now that I went from one crazy adrenaline rush another and then, there was seemingly nothing. Adrenaline is a chemical game in the body, and I'm not a doctor, but I believe when that chemical is not going through your body as often you go through a type of withdrawal.

I was fortunate to have found a very cool church and was able to join a musicians' club. A bit of a side note: While I was stationed in San Francisco, whenever I had a Sunday off duty, I would go to a place called Aquatic Park. At the park, a group of people would gather together, an odd mixture of people, like the president of Wells Fargo bank and Joe Blow on the street. They had a very cool drum circle with the addition of a bass guitar made of one string, a stick, and a pail. I would go every Sunday I could, and after being there so often I got to know some of the guys, and one of the men there taught me the basics of playing congas.

Fast forward, one day while at this new church, they said they were going to form a new musicians' club and if we played an instrument, we should come to the club. So I went. I was really having a hard time in my inner world and I thought maybe this would help. I brought my guitar because I had one and I could kind of play it. No coincidence though, when I got there one of the instructors had a set of congas. When it got to my turn to talk about myself and my choice of instrument I was able to tell them that, although I brought my guitar, I really wanted to play congas. So they taught me.

When I think about that time, it took a lot of energy to muster up enough courage to go to that club meeting. I remember being extremely uncomfortable walking out the door of my house, but with my roommate's encouragement to go, I went. Rarely do any of us take on something new without the encouragement of others. And so, with that, I was able to look forward to something each week. Something that seemed to feed my soul.

I could have talked about going to that class for a long time, but with encouragement, I actually went. When it comes to any great endeavor, adventure, or rescue, there always comes that time for execution. After all the planning and plotting, if a mountain is to be climbed, sooner or later the ascent must begin in order to get to the top. After all the years of knowing that change needed to happen, the time came to stop imagining the monsters I had created in my mind about telling my story. I had to end the constant recital of the "what ifs" that went on in my mind about counseling and therapy, these things that constituted "change" and the fears of telling my secrets.

I had to figure out how to muster up a different application of bravery. If the definition of courage or bravery is moving forward into uncertainty, risk, or emotional exposure, then somehow I needed to figure out a way to move forward into the uncertainty of my emotional world. Just as I did that first night as a rescue swimmer, where the survival of another human being in treacherous waters was "on me," or the seemingly simple act of walking out my door to that group of musicians. I had to use my ability to set aside my discomfort, to put my fears aside. I needed to reach inside myself and decide to jump into the scary unknown perils of my mind, to once again set aside my discomfort and fear, to initiate the rescue of the lost soul within me.

As a physiotherapist, while introducing my clients to a new technology in pain reduction, I noticed there was a lot of resistance to this new protocol. Even when people are in physical pain and there is something that has been scientifically proven to reduce that pain, still they resist. In the early days of that new technology it was very difficult to persuade people to give it a chance to ease their pain. Well, here I was in a time when post-traumatic stress was at the forefront of my mind with well-documented studies on how counseling and therapy can help. Still, I resisted this aid that could ease my emotional pain.

You know when you finally realize that it's time to do what needs to be done? I knew deep inside that I needed to take a chance on something new, at least something new to me. Just like the people who took a chance on that new technology. I would tell these people that they are so brave to step out of their comfort zone. Bravery really is all around us. We have no idea what other people are going through day to day. How many people do we encounter daily who are emotionally or physically spent? They are literally just getting through each day. That is bravery.

It was time to take a chance and step into the newness of letting someone help me with my pain. To allow someone to "see" me, to allow someone else into the dark void of my emotions. A place I had only gone to alone, and at that, seldom. I was a rookie once again and not a young one, embarking on learning new skills and applications of new tools. Only this time these skills and tools would be used to save *my* life, not someone else's.

One of my earliest challenges in this new endeavor was getting over issues of trust. Trust, by definition, is a reliance on the character, ability, strength, or truth of someone *in whom confidence is placed.* I was certainly lacking in the ability to place confidence in a complete stranger for my survival. Kind of like that man who was not all that happy to see me as his rescuer. He didn't have a lot of confidence that I could actually help. It was now my turn to put trust in someone else. I was the one who was cold, disoriented, worn out, and completely out of my element. Even though I felt as though I was too far away for any rescue, I believe God gave me strength enough to hope one more time. I made a choice to stop pushing the pain down and I was now ready and willing to be rescued.

The willingness to do what it takes for however long it takes is another big component. The same energy or willpower I would use to push pain and trauma away was the same energy I could tap into to bring it up and work through it. There's a great saying from Winston Churchill during WWII: "If you're going through hell, keep going." Hell is not a place to stop. I was already parked in a "hell" for too long and I knew that once I started *this* journey I wanted to continue to move through the pain, not stopping until the focus could move from addressing issues to moving into growth.

I have to say that I was fascinated by how fast help arrived when I let go of the controls and was willing to trust. I have a wonderful friend; he is a Vietnam veteran, he served in CAP units (USMC), and those who know him call him Doc. He is also a purple heart recipient. He certainly has been a godsend to me and to many more people, as I have come to learn. After we had spoken about my newfound status at Veterans Affairs, he offered to take me to the local VA so I could finish the process of getting into their system. This simple act of kindness was extremely uncomfortable for me to accept, but Doc was understanding, albeit stern. He said I *will* pick you up and take you there. He knew all too well that as easy as it is to say "yeah, I'll go," it is just as easy to not go. This was my first opportunity to put my choice to step out of my comfort zone into action, one of many opportunities ahead.

The idea of going to a facility that had anything to do with the military or my service made me very uneasy. Again, Doc was very aware of this. So he came and picked me up and we spent most of the day there, Doc quietly by my side as if to say, "You're not alone." That day was a gift I will never forget, and to Doc, I will be forever grateful. He made that trip himself many years back, he understood where my mind was, and all these years after Vietnam, this guy is still saving lives one trip to the VA at a time.

Part of being brave, especially this new understanding of brave, is a willingness to learn. This sounds obvious, but learning is a type of vulnerability. Putting myself in the position of learning means that I am willing to say I don't know. I didn't have the answers. I didn't even have many questions. I had no idea what this experience was going to be like and I was doing everything I could to keep my imagination at bay. To take each encounter without judgment. I only hoped that someone would be kind and be able to break through the outer defenses and through the numbness. I hoped there was enough of a heart and soul to be salvaged.

At my first interview, I was encouraged to do a class. I can remember, as if it was yesterday, the feeling in my gut. "Really? A class?" I don't like groups. I actually told the person I was talking to that I didn't like groups. I asked her why I couldn't just talk to someone. I told her that she was nice, perhaps I could talk to her... Not so much. There is a "process." But of course, I wasn't fond of that word. I just kept telling myself to breathe—still, I didn't like groups.

Group therapy was not on my radar, nor was it anything that interested me. The idea of listening to the pains that others had gone through was not what I had in mind. I had to, once again, remind myself of the man I rescued, the guy who was angry because this little girl was there to rescue him. Group class was not the package I wanted. But they, the facilitators at Veterans Affairs were trained well on how to help those with my particular needs, and so group therapy it was. Much to my surprise, I was not thrown into a group like I had imagined where everyone just spews their pains on everyone in attendance. They had rules, interestingly these rules made me feel like maybe it wouldn't be as bad as I thought it would be.

There is a fear and a freedom in vulnerability. Fear almost always precedes freedom. I can remember the "butterflies in the stomach" you know, like the feeling before you jump from high places or each time I jumped into the water, always a bit of nervousness before going out on a case. It was, however, in some way attached to excitement. The sensation of a nervous stomach was very familiar to me when I was doing something physical. That feeling was not so familiar and was more of a discomfort when attached to my emotional world.

The anticipation of being totally vulnerable with perfect strangers made my first time jumping into dark and angry water seems like a day at the beach. I think about the a conversation about jumping and was given this tip remember to hold yourself tight and breathe." I thought it was kind of odd that he would say this. I mean, of course you have to breathe...

I learned very quickly that it takes a long time to get to the water when jumping into uncertainty. I had done my share of jumping off of high dives and cliffs when I was younger. The highest cliff I jumped off of as a teenager was close to sixty-five feet, into water of course. But jumping into uncertain conditions and peril, you need to take a big deep breath, you actually need to breathe while you are in freefall especially when that freefall is in your mind. When my friend told me to breathe, He was so very right. It has been one of my great takeaways from those years and it's all I remember, while in freefall—*BREATHE*.

It also takes time to reorganize the scars of trauma, so I remembered to breathe and continue to. It seems so simple, breathing, and yet doesn't it seem like when we need to breathe the most, we tend to hold our breath? When we are scared, we tend to hold our breath. When exercising, many people hold their breath during the movements. Many of my clients while being treated will hold their breath, and I constantly remind them to breathe. We all do it, when we feel vulnerable or scared or in pain. It is a way we try to protect ourselves. My encouragement, if you ever entering into a scary or painful place: Breathe. While in freefall, you have to breathe. It is necessary to get you through to the next step.

CHAPTER 8

Trust the Process

P rocess. At some point in time and for some unknown reason, I had decided that a process was a messy and unnecessary delay. I don't know where that belief came from and why I held on to it for so long, when everything that we have ever learned is due to a process. If ever we want to master something, we need to begin a process that will lead us to mastery.

There is a saying I've always liked: "All masters were once a disaster." I remember an anecdote that was related to this saying. Some people learn to ski and some people just learn how to get down the mountain safely. There is a BIG difference between the two. The goals are the same really, to get down the mountain. The *way* someone gets down the mountain and the journeys, if you will, are different. When getting down the mountain safely, the underlying goal is getting to the bottom of the hill *without getting hurt*. When learning to really ski, the goal is to come to some higher skill level up to mastery. With each step up into the higher mastery of more complicated terrain, there will be more risk, and with that the possibility of injury increases. It is a price of mastering a physical skill and the only way to that mastery.

In my early years as both an athlete and as a Coast Guard swimmer, I would consider myself someone who had the desire to master skills. Athletic skills, for sure, as I had very high athletic intelligence. Physical injuries were never a hinderance to me. I understood the risks and was absolutely willing to take those risks for the purpose of becoming as good as I could at each particular skill. What I didn't understand, and perhaps one of the purposes of this book, was that I was not aware of the emotional risks. I was young, strong (for a "little" girl), and had a determined mindset, just as so many helpers, heroes, and warriors who have come before and after me. But these unforeseen, subconscious emotional insults were not on my radar. Even though I had my share of trauma, I had no idea that those early traumas of being burned were only the beginning of many building blocks to come.

Emotional wounds have been such taboo, even as late as the 1980s, that it wasn't even in wide address until the last fifteen years or so. It is said that A. A. Milne wrote the books about Winnie the Pooh to help him relate to his son Christopher about the effects of post-traumatic stress from his service in WWI and WWII, with characters such as Eeyore who represented the depression he felt, Piglet representing anxiety, and Tigger representing mania. Back then it was called "shell shock." These insults have had many names; it is now documented as post-traumatic stress.

Being a disaster is humbling. Especially, when there has been some mastery in other places in one's life or when someone has been in a place of authority. It is humbling for someone who is a bit more advanced in age to be a disaster. So much self-judgment around not having it together enough or that all familiar "I should know this stuff." They say, "You can't teach an old dog new tricks." Actually, you can, but the old dog must be willing to learn. Pride is another type of self-inflicted prison. I know for me, fear, ego, and unhealthy pride were big factors that kept me from allowing myself to express the disaster within to those who were close.

It seems like there are so many challenges that keep us from achieving our hopes and dreams. Someone once said that dreams are goals without plans. Plans or processes are the only way to really achieve any goal. When I was in the midst of going to the Trauma Skills Group, I would say out loud to myself, "Trust the process." It was my mantra. Even though I didn't really trust anyone or anything, I chose to keep taking steps. Those first few weeks were somewhat traumatic in and of themselves, as part of the process was to look at how I was reacting to situations in my own life.

Definitions have become a lifeline for me during this time, in that they give my mind facts to work with rather than the made-up stories in my head. We were given many definitions in that group and they were a great source of comfort for me. The definition of process is "a natural phenomenon marked by gradual changes that lead toward a particular result." The key takeaways for me from this definition were "natural" and "gradual changes." This is a very different definition from the one that I had made up in my mind. It's also a different experience to think about process from a proactive mindset verses a reactive one. I am fascinated by how easily I can take something I had actually "made up in my mind" to be so much bigger and more daunting than it really is. Natural, gradual change. I can do that.

The truth of the matter is we are all constantly in a process. Learning is a constant in this life. We are always taking new information into our brains. If we are constantly feeding and filling our mind with negative content, then more than likely negative content will take hold of our subconscious and we will become that person who always finds the negative in any situation. Same with positive input. We are what we absorb. Mindset is based on what we absorb; absorption happens when we saturate our mind, with the combination of mindset, either negative or positive we will eventually lean toward that which we are feeding our mind.

Something I've learned over my years in the healing arts is that certain vitamins and minerals are absorbed better by the body when they are in combination with other vitamins or minerals. For instance, the human body absorbs turmeric better when it is mixed with black pepper. Certain kinds of calcium absorb better when combined with magnesium. So we are not what we eat, we are what we absorb. The right combination, of a healthy process of understanding post-traumatic stress and a positive setting in which to present it can and usually does create gradual positive changes for those who learn to trust the process.

This trusting the process is like an athlete finally wrapping their head around the fact that they need to take time off in order to heal. An athlete with an injury can engage in one of two processes. The athlete can either have a process in place to rehabilitate the injured area OR continue a process of not addressing the injury and sooner than later that athlete will not be able to play. The healing only comes when we stop doing the activity or activities that created or aggravates the injury. When dealing with an acute injury, the protocol is: As immediately as possible, begin "RICE" (rest, ice, compression, elevation). Recently, new research has suggested adding "movement" to this protocol, because lack of movement or motion can completely lock up a joint or muscle. While working with my clients, I would instruct them to do as much movement as possible at home without creating more pain. In other words, be an active participant in the healing process. The end result of addressing an injury sooner than later and following the protocol completely has proven that the active participant always has a much shorter rehabilitation period. Completing the protocol and continuing to strengthen (that is, continuing the process which includes strength conditioning) is imperative.

Participation. Being an active participant in the healing process. This really hit home with me as it has been something that I have emphasized in my business for years. I have said to each and every client that they have a lot of power in this process. The more they participate in their "homework," the faster they will recover. It is ALWAYS those who are willing to participate and do the homework who recover faster and more completely. Those who were willing to do what it took even if there was frustration, pain, and limitations. They chose to do the work.

When I became aware that it was time for me to start the process of healing my invisible wounds, this instruction of being an active participant became my focus, meaning I had to focus and will myself to participate. I remember sitting in my first Trauma Skills Group and having an epic battle in my mind to stay present. I didn't participate much that first class, but I vowed to go to every class. That's not to say I didn't battle every week to get myself there. I would tell myself out loud, "What if you were going to physical therapy, you'd go to that, right? OK then, just get to class and trust the process."

This was my time when I looked in the mirror and said, "If I want different results, it is time to do something different." Not to read yet another book safely in solitude. I needed to take a risk on this process. I needed to look at my reactions to my present experiences. If only because, even after reading all the books and studying all I could, the simple act of someone cutting me off in traffic revealed that the anger monster hadn't been slain, the smallest insult could stir that monster into an instantaneous rage. Reactions tell the stories of the subconscious. Reactions tell the stories of our past.

I read a lot of books and learned a lot about managing my emotions. I learned about meditation and prayer. I learned a lot about the effects of food and alcohol on the mind, body, and emotions. I studied philosophy, neurolinguistics, and self-hypnosis among other things. I was trying to grow, but being in a constant state of survival, "fight, flight or freeze," I was exhausted. Everything was based on my terms, my comfort level, and my ability to navigate what I was feeling. So, I circled back to not having the tools within myself to navigate feelings that were buried.

My crossroads came often. The response for so long was to read some more books or take another online class, of course in the comfort of solitude. I had this opportunity now where I could be brave and really see myself and let myself be seen by others. To start a new adventure into a place that is the equivalent to me of a really scary movie with ghosts and monsters jumping out of hidden places. This is not a movie. As I have learned, the monsters can only scare me in the dark, when they are hidden. Once they are exposed and in the light, they lose their power. They are no longer these all-powerful and consuming entities. They are, however, layers of injuries and pains that, with kindness, understanding and guidance, can dissipate.

Keep breathing. Jumping out of the door of a helicopter for the first time is absolutely and literally breathtaking. It is extremely hard to breathe when doing something so new and scary. Each time I did it, though, I found it easier to breathe in the semi-controlled state of chaos known as freefall. Stepping into this unknown place of therapy felt like freefall. A semi-controlled state of emotional chaos, an absolutely perfect description of these next steps in my life. Making a choice to start looking at the past in order to move forward. To step into a process and to follow through with that process.

My encouragement when in this place, this crossroads, this awareness of choice: Be brave, be honest when you look in the mirror, and be kind to yourself. Allow yourself to be seen, even if it's with one person. Do it. Be wise in your choosing of that person, of course. You won't regret it. This is the beginning of creating a powerful place for real growth. The challenge in this place is to stay focused. Be a part of the process. We all have great power as participants in our healing.

CHAPTER 9

Distractions

San Francisco Bay is extremely large. Think, if you will, of the Grand Canyon, and then put water in it. Oh, and a couple of islands just to make it interesting. It is easy to get lost there if you don't know how to navigate. There are many fast and confused currents, along with times of big winds. I learned a lot of lessons on that big beautiful bay, albeit many of those lessons were not realized or understood till much later in my life. Some lessons were simpler and kinder than others. Every time I went out on the water, I learned something. In hindsight and reflection, I learned a lot about what I was capable of; I also realized breaking points. As I recall the rescues, the situations and perils, I am fascinated with how many of those lessons were repetitive, those that seeped into my subconscious and how, with the help of some great emotional navigators, those lessons are becoming clearer each day.

When it comes to the healing process in general there are different phases and milestones. The moment an injury happens is the best time possible to address it. Unfortunately, it is seldom that we are able to work with someone at the immediate time of injury. If someone comes to see me within days of an injury when it is new, the injury is known and it is more easily and effectively treated. As we have discussed though, most of the time people tend to do the "wait and see" approach to injuries. I used to think that the wait-and-see approach was a viable approach, but in reality every injury, however small, leaves its mark.

Now, when I have a small incident or accident or when I know someone who has had a recent injury, my advice is to at the very least address the injury with some kind of treatment. Ultimately, it would be best to do what you would do for a bigger injury. It can't hurt and it will most definitely help speed up the healing process and decrease the time in pain. So even with the smallest sprain or strain of any sort, "RICEM." **R**est, **I**ce, **C**ompress (if applicable), **E**levate, and start minimal **M**ovement within the confines of not creating more pain. This will always facilitate a faster recovery with minimal scar tissue, which in turn results in a better chance of full recovery. As we have discussed, emotional injuries are a reflection of physical injuries. Imagine if we approached the pains of our souls as we do the pains of our bodies. From the smallest to the most horrendous insults, if we were to address them sooner than later, how much time and pain we would be able to save ourselves.

The lessons I learned in San Francisco were not all from rescues, as the Coast Guard is charged with marine safety and law enforcement as well as safety of life at sea. We also worked with a very young organization at the time, called the Environmental Protection Agency. The Coast Guard back then, however, was considered the law of the water. We were constantly on the lookout for either drug labs on barges or drug smugglers coming into the Bay on boats. In the eighties there was so much drug activity that we had DEA briefings and printouts of suspect boats. Many nights while on duty we would sit under the Golden Gate Bridge for hours looking for these DEA-targeted boats. The hours I spent while on duty were many times combined, law enforcement with search and rescue. A very large amount of the law enforcement in those days was drug interdiction. So it would be very safe to say that every boat crew member in San Francisco was on high alert for anything that "smelled" of drug running.

One late afternoon, my boat crew received a call about a man threatening to jump off of one of the prominent bridges in the area. We were informed that all local first responders had been notified and were either on scene or in route to the scene. "Jumpers" required all hands on deck. The sheriff's department was there, usually the highway patrol as they took care of bridge traffic, local police, and the fire Department—all present during a call in for a jumper.

As my boat crew and I arrived on scene we could see with our binoculars the bridge and the potential jumper. He was over the rails and standing on ledge of the bridge. We could see the highway patrol and the sheriff, and we saw both fire and police departments doing their part to get this man off of the bridge. We could see there was a lot of tension between the first responders and the jumper—pretty standard. Along with tension, there is a lot of *attention* that goes with someone attempting to jump off a bridge. Traffic is a mess, a lot of manpower is diverted to the scene, media usually shows up, and it creates controlled chaos. One could say it creates a great distraction to the routines of a day. The manpower that we would normally have allocated to law enforcement patrols must divert to the scene of the jumper. That means that those resources aren't able to do anything else, and it leaves the rest of the Bay Area with what would amount to a skeleton crew to handle all other traffic or emergency needs. It's hard to describe how one person could divert so much attention away from other needs in the city or on the water.

Without going into a lot of detail here, we were very aware that there were those who "threaten" to jump off a bridge for attention. Those people usually stand down safely and uneventfully once the media shows up. When someone is on the bridge for hours, and definitely long after the media is on scene, something is not right—they are looking for much more than attention. This was usually a deliberate distraction to divert regular patrols and regular duties, thus leaving holes in the safety blanket of law enforcement, leaving the Bay vulnerable to other elicit activities.

This rescue or "stand-off" was going nowhere and time was just passing away. Our boat crew started to talk amongst ourselves and concluded that this guy was just wasting our time and had no real intent to jump off of that bridge. We had to stay; this was our duty at this point in time. The question was, why would anyone want to waste not only the California Highway Patrol's time, but the sheriff, police, and fire departments as well as the U.S. Coast Guard's time? Why else? As long as the focus was on the jumper, it would not be on any vehicles. Boats, cars, and trucks bring tons of drugs into the Bay Area. Unfortunately, this was so normal in the eighties that our thoughts were constantly on alert for this kind of activity. Deception and Distractions were all part of the game.

Distractions abound more now than any other time in history. Between social media, when I'm feeling reclusive, to full-on filling time with people, TV, or burying myself in work. I recall when I was deciding to start the group therapy classes, the time when the rubber was meeting the road, I had to pick the days and times that I was going to commit to going to these classes. I came up with so many things that I *could* do instead of these classes. Not that I was actually doing anything at that particular time of day other than sleeping, but I "could" work out, yeah, that would be good for me, or I "could" get up early and go for a walk each morning. Again, I wasn't doing those things. I was, however, semi-depressed and just wanted to sleep in rather than get up and workout or get ready for a class I was not looking forward to at eight in the morning.

I realized that if I was really interested in seeing what my life could look like other than the smallness in which I was living, then I needed to bite the bullet and commit to going to these classes. I told myself that I needed to give this a chance, just as if I had a physical injury.

I needed to at least start a protocol and commit to it. If one protocol doesn't work, then I need to find another until I find the one that does. I would do this for a physical injury, so I decided that I must do this for my emotional life as well. I mean, what good is it to be in great physical condition and not have the emotional fortitude to be able to interact socially? I've been doing that for years, great physical health but really no progress relationally.

There are all kinds of distractions: physical distractions, pains, and accidental injuries that can interrupt our routines and keep us from certain plans or goals. These are usually more annoying and things that slow us down, but at some point we are able to get back into routine. Then there are what I call emotional distractions. These are the things that keep us from moving forward in life. We all have them. The television, which used to be something that brought families together decades ago, has become the great mind numb and subliminal marketing tool of the century. Not to say that there isn't some great content in television. But I would admit that it has been a great escape for me, even in the name of education.

There are social and intellectual distractions as well. In truth, there are so many potential distractions that I was able to bounce from one distraction to another for years. One such distraction came disguised as "personal growth." I did and still do a lot of personal development. But back when I had an understanding that I needed to "change" and knew I didn't have the emotional tools to create that change, I would "distract" myself with some personal growth book and put a Band-Aid on my wound. I could bury myself in a self-help book and get some great information, rather than taking a risk and exposing my emotional self to someone. That said, all of those books have been invaluable on this journey. With the things I have learned through therapy, those books and the information they contain now REALLY make sense, and I now have the ability to apply that instruction.

I have found that when it came right down to it, I truly wanted to *be* more and *do* more with the life that I have been given, and distractions were and are a great battleground. Back to those first group classes, I came up with so many distractions to keep me from "doing the work", whether it be a reading assignment, a worksheet, or meditation. Every time I would get ready to meditate, my mind would be all over the place, anywhere but present. I could find *anything* to do other than do the homework that was assigned. I would clean my house and I really don't like to clean my house, but it was better than looking at the homework that was ultimately exposing the things I wanted to change.

The thing that always brought me back to those crossroads and doing the homework was a desire for peace in my soul and quietness in my mind. The lack of which was the telltale that no matter how many seminars I attended or books I read, there was still this low-grade irritation, this constant noise in my head. The birthplace of outbursts of anger and bouts of depression. So this was really the driving force keeping me in the process of healing. This is what initially brought me to a desire to commit to the classes. They had a step-by-step process, and they were very aware of where I was at each step. They were the experts and they were there to help.

My awareness of distractions is very high these days. It doesn't matter what the distraction looks like or where it comes from. What matters is that I can identify them for what they do. What they do is keep me away from priorities—the important things in life. What is important? Actually, that which is of the highest importance is very simple. It is a matter of answering one question: What do you want? "What do you want" can be looked at like planning a big event. After all, when it comes to this life, as an individual, understanding what I want is actually the biggest event of my life. Well, first and foremost I wanted the noise in my head to stop. I wanted the anger to go away and I wanted the constant internal irritability to be gone.

So if I were planning an event, I would start to look at the first things I need to do. The very first thing I needed was a date for this event. With a date it actually made the event real. In order to make this event happen, I needed to put a task list together. I had to make some financial, social, and emotional choices. I had to step out of my comfort zone and do something different to get different results. I had to decide that this time, I wasn't just going to read about change, but I was going to seek out someone or some organization to help me create change. We have a saying amongst my sailing friends regarding taking action. "We're in dog years." Meaning, simply, time is much shorter now than ever it was, so if I am going to do something, now would be a good time to do it, because we are in dog years. Our time on this planet, no matter how old we are, is limited.

The story of the jumper. When someone is truly intent on bringing about change, they usually do it very quickly. That is, when the decision is made then the steps are taken more swiftly. The choices become swifter the closer we get to realizing what we really want. When the intent is to change, we are no longer seeking attention or creating a distraction like with the jumper.

The hardest part about making a change is the process of deciding. Once the decision is made, all energy is diverted to executing the plan, focused on the actual process of change, step by step with as few distractions as possible.

CHAPTER 10

Stay the Course

L ife is short. We hear this all the time. People say it in passing, people say it as almost a throwaway sentence, but the bottom line is we are here on earth for what amounts to a heartbeat. Even though I have great faith that there's something on the other side, the truth of the matter is nobody knows what our next adventure is. What we do know is that we have this time here and now and if we are intent on being present with family and friends, or if we want to make some greater contribution other than simply existing, then we must ask ourselves some questions. We touched on the big question in the last chapter. It has been and continues to be a deep and evasive question to answer. Partially because it evolves. For instance, a very simple example would be: *It's a hot day, I want some frozen yogurt.* Simple, but how many subconscious questions come from going into the yogurt shop, and how many subconscious decisions do we make while there? Yes, I'm in the yogurt shop, now what? I must decide what size cup, what flavor yogurt, how many toppings and which ones. All these little choices to create the yogurt I want. The big question from the beginning is, "What do I want?"

I read a billboard recently that said most people spend more time planning a vacation than they do planning their retirement. That was eye-opening! I have come to believe we do this partially because, really, no one wants to believe we will ever get old, but also I think we haven't been educated to ask certain questions. Somehow goals have become obscured in the shadows of distractions. All great inventions, development, and growth have come from asking great questions. The great question I like to ask myself about many things, throughout the day even, is: "What do I want?" I started doing this as I became aware that most of the time I was running on autopilot, doing the same things over and over again with no new outcomes, no goals other than getting through the day without incident. Which, while in the midst of fight, flight, or freeze is a great accomplishment in and of itself. Asking the question ("What do I want"?) put me in a more powerful position for not only personal enlightenment, but it gave pause in any situation to think before reacting. It has helped me to slow down enough to assess my choices, helped me to stay true to my intentions in life, and ultimately helped me achieve my goals for each day and for the bigger picture of my life. Goals can be as simple as the perfect yogurt for a beautiful day or as grand as choosing to stay home and write because I want to finish writing this book.

Once we hear truth, we can never unhear it. What we choose to do with truth is a personal journey. I believe every human on this planet has a purpose. Purpose cannot be measured, as it too is relative to individuals, beliefs, intentions, and desires. I have come to learn, however, that if someone is intent on doing something specific, being purposeful in this life, or wanting things to change, then that person must begin by asking the great question, "What do I want?" It is not asked lightly or once or twice, it is a very deep and thoughtful pursuit to understand what "what do I want" means to me. It is a question to ask regarding relationships, jobs, careers, vacations, and again, the big picture of life.

Once I can answer the question of "what do I want" in any particular realm of my world, then the other big question is: "What am I willing to do to bring that about"? Of course, legally, ethically, and morally.

Am I willing to let my time on earth slip away without doing the things that make me feel alive, without doing the things that make me feel as though I have a purpose, without doing the things that give me joy, pure and simple, joy? If I want to experience a pure and simple joy, what am I willing to do to get it? Am I willing to explore the depths of my mind and heart to see what's hindering me? Am I willing to explore the depths of my soul and the fears and the pains and the traumas and the injuries and the insults? Or maybe it's a simple as this: "Am I willing to step out of my comfort zone to plan for that trip of a lifetime? What *am* I willing to do?" These are fair questions for each of us to ask ourselves. Am I willing to explore those things, with the reward being breakthroughs, dreams realized, loving and kind relationships, joy, inner peace, and becoming the person I know I was born to be?

Staying the course in nautical terms is a fast way of saying, "Do not alter the direction in which the ship is headed." This is used a lot in stormy weather or tumultuous seas. It is used when the direction we are going in feels like it could be dangerous or perhaps become rough or questionable as when a storm would suddenly come up. The captain will say to the navigator, "Stay the course."

Navigation on the open ocean is something that has fascinated me ever since I was introduced to it as a young Coast Guardswoman. To "plot a course" was to create "legs" or "headings" to follow in order to arrive at a desired destination and if all goes well, within a certain timeframe. Sometimes in plotting a course there are obstacles that need to be accounted for; very rarely is there ever a straight line from one place on the sea to another. As recently as the 1980s, there was no GPS; it didn't exist then. We would use a system called dead reckoning, short for deduced reckoning. Dead reckoning, also written as ded reckoning, is estimating the position of a vessel from its speed, direction of travel, and time elapsed, making use of compass and clock. The alternative to ded reckoning was pilotage, which made use of actual visible landmarks and celestial navigation by the Sun, the Moon, and stars. Pilotage, to me, was more of an "on the fly" kind of thing, where the course was corrected from what could be seen. A navigator would be directed by the captain to "take a fix"—that is, tell me where we are right now. Ded reckoning is a process by which we draw the headings we need to travel, mark those headings on a chart, and then, using time, speed, and distance traveled to deduce our whereabouts. This was the process I used to "take a fix", with correction for currents. I could tell my captain where we were instead of using pilotage. With ded reckoning we can plot an entire trip, and then, with corrections made for currents and wind, we could very closely estimate our time of arrival. This is a fairly simple explanation. (On long trips there can be many different headings or directions to travel in order to reach a specific destination.)

Sometimes in life, as on the open sea, we have to *go through* the storm. Sometimes, we must stay the course. Sometimes we don't have the option to avoid the storm, or to hide from the pains or inconvenience of the "storms." The storms of life are like some storms on the sea. Sometimes they surprise us, like when certain behaviors interrupt relationships, income, or social interaction.

I know there were many times I thought I had weathered every storm possible in my emotional life, but in reality I just got better and better at altering my course. Whenever a course is altered, the arrival time to the desired destination is delayed. Every time I would read another book or take another online course, although I gained some great information from that education, I was actually putting the cart before the horse and was delaying the arrival to more peace in my mind. I am thankful for the information that I gained from those books and courses, but it had its negative effects as well in that it fed the belief that I was incapable of changing.

I needed to first find a good "crew" to go with me on this journey. A team, if you will, of skilled people who knew how to navigate the waters of post-traumatic stress. That team would help to choose a good course based on my initial destination of understanding why I was reacting the way I was reacting to situations and life. Once I found that crew and course, I made a decision to stay on it. Each time there was a breakthrough, I was able to start another leg of the journey. I continue this process, finding new "legs" to plot on this journey because I choose to continue to evolve.

With each leg of this life journey, I become more able to make the necessary course corrections without being totally thrown off course by "storms" or unforeseen obstacles. I am able to make small corrections to keep me going in the right direction. When ded reckoning, an actual line is drawn on a chart, a line that represents the heading in which we are traveling. Every fifteen minutes, half hour, or on the hour, the navigator will "take a fix" to check in and see (deduce) where we are and make the necessary heading corrections to stay on course with each particular leg of the journey.

This is the same for having a process leading to an intended outcome. I chose the skilled professionals at Veterans Affairs Women's Mental Health Services as my "crew" and the Trauma Skills Group as my first leg of a great journey. Each week I had the opportunity to assess where I was on this journey and to make small corrections so as to stay on course. Small corrections, not huge course changes, to stay on course and arrive at the destination within a certain timeframe. It is much easier to plot a long journey when it is broken down into smaller legs of that journey. A phrase I've learned along the way is "chunking it down"—looking at the overall goal and breaking it into small milestones that finally lead to the end goal.

So many seemingly small phrases have come into such great light during this journey. And, mind you, I have come to enjoy this as a journey, as life, in my opinion, should be a journey. Some of the small phrases that have big impact like "baby steps" or "take it one step at a time." Phrases that some of us have heard all our life, but for me they were more of those throw away statements like "life is short." Perhaps it is my heightened awareness of growing older that has me looking at these phrases from the perspective of them being such profound truths.

It truly is the small intentional steps that add up to the achievement of all great things. The actor Will Smith talks about his upbringing and how his dad taught him how to build a brick wall. As Will says, and I'm paraphrasing a bit, "You don't set out to build a wall, you don't start there, you start by saying, 'I'm going to lay this brick as perfectly as a brick can be laid.' You do that every single day, and as you do that, you will have your wall."

Small steps do some amazing things. They allow us to create a track record of accomplishment, they help us build confidence in order to do bigger or more complicated things. I would never put a child on a bicycle with two wheels who had no experience doing that and say, "OK now, ride the bike." That would just be cruel. Step by step. This is how we learn; this is how we have always learned. On the other hand, when we look at something like a wall, big and beyond our under-standing, and how to bring it about—without smaller steps, it becomes overwhelming, frustrating, demoralizing, and defeating.

My journey really started when I finally realized how little involved I was and decided that I wanted to be free from what held me back from participating in my life. Free from what was holding me back from truly being "a part of" instead of being "apart from" my life and those in it. I decided I wanted to be present with family, friends, and others. I decided I wanted to be a part of something bigger than myself. My "what do I want" was answered. Funny how my goal in joining the Coast Guard was for that same purpose, to be a part of something bigger.

So, as with all great adventures, the first thing is to gather the team that will be a part of this expedition. There are many different organiza-tions available to look for teammates. As a veteran, the Veterans Affairs in my city was my first stop to find some tools that I would need along the way. Anxiety and Depression Association of America is a civilian organization, as well as many others. We are in some amazing times in that we have many resources online or by phone. But the most important thing is to choose to take some action. Small steps create great gains. Even starting with one person on the team can create amazing results. Letting someone in and allowing them to see you completely.

I think about two key people who helped me outside of my loving family and friends. Two key people who understood where I was, because they had been there. I would not have known about the second one without the first. My first teammate taught me about benefits I didn't know I had through Veterans Affairs, and the other literally drove me to the VA to help me stay the course. We need teammates, we are not created to walk this life alone. We are not created to live inside our mind without expression. There are people who are ready to help us get on a course to freedom and they are there to help us stay the course when there are storms.

This journey is not just from rescue to recovery—there is so much more beyond that. But just as on that first night in the San Francisco Bay, jumping into a black and stormy ocean with a lot of unknowns awaiting me, wrestling with the voices in my head, in that moment, I knew what I had to do. Stop thinking about it and jump.

CHARACTERISTICS

of Post-traumatic Stress and Resources

This is not a complete list of post-traumatic stress characteristics, but they are some of the very common ones. This is not a diagnosis, these are common symptoms. If many of these thoughts or feelings are true for you, then please, take the next step and tell someone, family, friends or professional.

- Difficulty falling asleep

- Nightmares/night terrors

- Unable to remember dreams

- Constantly irritable

- Easily angered to the extreme

- Constant stomach upset or tension

- Difficulty controlling anger
- Not able to tell others about experiences
- Feeling guilty without knowing why
- Moving from job to job
- Difficulty concentrating
- Difficulty remembering events
- Difficulty making or keeping friends
- Vivid memories of unpleasant events
- Restlessness
- Constant tension or anxiety
- Feeling detached emotionally numb
- No leisure activities
- Unable to express feelings
- Experience lack of social contact
- Suicidal thoughts
- Cannot feel close to family
- Jumping at slight noises
- Unable to relax
- Feeling emotionally numb
- Alcohol or drug abuse
- Feeling worthless

There are some great resources on the internet. One that has many resources within its website is the Anxiety and Depression Association of America (ADAA), an international nonprofit organization dedicated to the prevention, treatment, and cure of anxiety, depression, OCD, PTSD, and co-occurring disorders.

There are also many mobile apps that have been created to help with anxiety and relaxation. Go to your device's app store and search for mindfulness, relaxation, and meditation. These are in no way a substitute for professional counseling. They are, however, great in conjunction with counseling.

ABOUT THE AUTHOR

Tracey Brown is a United States Coast Guard Veteran 1983-1987 QM3. She wore many hats as most Coast Guard men and women did in those days. She would be a firefighter one day, a small boat crew swimmer another. The Quartermaster rating in the USCG specializes in navigation. Even before understanding the extent of how the characteristics of PTSD had affected her personal life, Tracey was educated as a Director of Physical Rehabilitation and has been working for over twenty five years in the field. The last decade has been dedicated to specialized work in pain reduction via scar tissue therapy. This is where she began to realize the "lostness" and confusion PTSD can create. Her hope is to help not only the helpers, heroes and warriors get beyond the stigma of PTSD but for *all* that have endured stress after trauma and hopes to help further the conversation and understanding of Post-traumatic Stress.